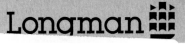

GW00367213

BUSINESS LISTENING AND SPEAKING

PRE-INTERMEDIATE

David Riley

Contents

Introduction to the learner

Business Listening and Speaking Pre-intermediate is the first of two books to help you develop your English listening and speaking skills in a business context.

Objectives

You can use the book even if your level of English is only basic. It will help you to understand what you hear and to practise some of the language yourself.

The material

You can use the book on your own or with a teacher. There are two audio cassettes with the book and you should use the book with the cassettes. The cassettes contain all the model conversations and practice exercises. Everything on the cassettes is marked 🖭 in the book. If you want to record your answers, you will need a second cassette recorder and a blank cassette.

Using the material

There are twelve units in the book. Each unit has five sections:

A Preparation
This section introduces the situation and some of the important vocabulary in the unit.

B Listening
This section helps you to understand spoken English. There are questions and exercises to check your understanding.

C Language check
This section teaches you new language (grammar and vocabulary) and practises language you have met before.

D Pronunciation
Most of these sections practise English stress in words and sentences. There is also some work on intonation. Part of each Pronunciation section is a shadow reading exercise. You must speak **at the same time** as the voice on the cassette. You may find it difficult at first but keep practising – it is a very good way of improving your spoken English. You may have to do these exercises many times before you get them right.

E   Speaking

This section gives you the opportunity to use all the new language you have learned in the unit.

Answer key

There is an Answer key at the end of the book. The Answer key has the scripts of all the material recorded on the cassettes and the answers to most of the exercises. In some exercises you will give your opinion or give information about yourself or your company. When this happens there are no answers in the Answer key.

The phonemic scripts

Business Listening and Speaking uses the phonemic script because it is helpful with English pronunciation. Did you know that from the five vowels in English (a, e, i, o, u) we can make twenty different sounds?

Here are the phonemic sounds which English uses and an example word for each one.

vowels

/æ/	flat	/flæt/	/ə/	better	/ˈbetər/	/i/	three	/θriː/	/uː/ soon /suːn/
/aː/	car	/kɑːr/	/ɜː/	earn	/ɜːn/	/ɒ/	what	/wɒt/	/ɔː/ caught /kɔːt/
/e/	head	/hed/	/ɪ/	six	/sɪks/	/ʊ/	book	/bʊk/	/ʌ/ cut /kʌt/

diphthongs

time	/taɪm/	employ	/ɪmˈplɔɪ/	here	/hɪər/	now /naʊ/
name	/neɪm/	there	/ðeər/	fuel	/fʊəl/	go /gəʊ/

consonants

/b/	big	/big/	/h/	hot	/hot/	/p/	plan	/plæn/	/θ/	think	/θɪŋk/
/k/	call	/kɔːl/	/dʒ/	just	/dʒʌst/	/r/	road	/rəʊd/	/v/	very	/verɪ/
/tʃ/	change	/tʃeɪndʒ/	/l/	like	/laɪk/	/s/	seven	/sevən/	/w/	wet	/wet/
/d/	desk	/desk/	/m/	make	/meɪk/	/ʃ/	ship	/ʃɪp/	/y/	yes	/jes/
/f/	fine	/faɪn/	/n/	no	/nəʊ/	/t/	ten	/ten/	/z/	zone	/zəʊn/
/g/	get	/get/	/ŋ/	thing	/θɪŋ/	/ð/	this	/ðɪs/	/ʒ/	measure	/meʒər/

Before you start

When you meet a new word in *Business Listening and Speaking* you can use an English only dictionary, for example, *The Longman Active Study Dictionary of English*, or a bilingual dictionary (English and your language) to check the meaning. In some sections of the book it is very important for you to understand the meaning of new words before you continue with an exercise. You will see 📖 which means that you should check the meaning of any new words in a dictionary before you continue. When you meet a new word in *Business Listening and Speaking* make a note of it in a vocabulary book or file. It is a good idea to write an example sentence which shows you how the word is used. It is also a good idea to mark the stress.

Arriving for an appointment

Language for
arriving at reception for an appointment
giving and understanding directions

1A Preparation

1. Answer these questions.

   a. Do you usually arrive for dinner at a friend's house:
      i. a little early?
      ii. exactly on time?
      iii. a little late?

   b. When people arrive ten or fifteen minutes late for a business meeting, do you feel:
      i. angry?
      ii. a little angry?
      iii. perfectly all right?

   c. What is the earliest time of day you normally have a business meeting?

   d. What is the latest time of day you normally have a business meeting?

2. Now you will hear Jill Warburton, a director of a British publishing company, answering the same questions.

   Listen to cassette 1A.2 and read silently.

When you're having dinner at a friend's house, do you usually try to arrive on time, or a little late, or...?
For dinner, a little late. Maybe fifteen minutes, not more than half an hour: it gives people time if anything's gone wrong.

What about if people arrive late for a business meeting, say ten or fifteen minutes. How do you feel about that?
Mm. That's different. No, I don't like that. I expect people to arrive on time for business meetings.

What's the earliest time of day you normally have a business meeting?
Normally nine-thirty. Nine if it's really necessary, for example, if someone comes on an early flight.

And the latest?
Five o'clock. I finish work at six, though I sometimes work later.

1B Listening

Listen to cassette 1B.

You will hear four conversations. In each conversation a visitor is arriving at reception for an appointment.

Play the conversations as many times as you want and answer the questions.

1. Look at the chart. Which visitor is seeing which manager at what time?

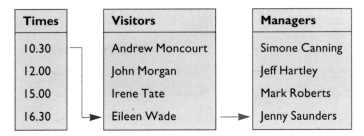

Times	Visitors	Managers
10.30	Andrew Moncourt	Simone Canning
12.00	John Morgan	Jeff Hartley
15.00	Irene Tate	Mark Roberts
16.30	Eileen Wade	Jenny Saunders

2. Complete the table.
  a. Which visitors are on time?
  b. Which visitors are late? Why?
  c. Which visitors have to wait? How long?

	a. on time	b. late and reason why	c. waiting time
Andrew Moncourt	✓		
John Morgan			
Irene Tate			
Eileen Wade			

3. Where are these offices? Write on the floor plans.
  a. Simone Canning's office
  b. Jeff Hartley's office
  c. Mark Roberts's office
  d. Jenny Saunders's office

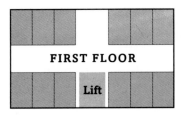

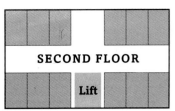

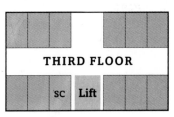

Check your answers in the key **1B**

1C Language check

📖 Vocabulary

Use the words in the box to complete this conversation.
Write one word in each space.

afraid appointment expecting floor free help lift name office wait

RECEPTIONIST Good morning. Can I .... you?

VISITOR Yes. I've got an .... with Annette Rawstern.

RECEPTIONIST What time is she .... you?

VISITOR Ten o'clock.

RECEPTIONIST Could I have your .... , please?

VISITOR John Wilson.

RECEPTIONIST Take a seat. I'll see if she's ....

VISITOR Thank you.

RECEPTIONIST I'm .... she's on the phone at the moment. Could you .... a few minutes?

VISITOR Certainly.

(a few minutes later)

RECEPTIONIST You can go up now. Do you know where her .... is?

VISITOR Er, no.

RECEPTIONIST It's on the third .... Come out of the .... , turn right and it's the second on the left.

VISITOR Thank you.

RECEPTIONIST Not at all.

📼 Now listen to cassette 1C.

Check your answers in the key **1C**

1D Pronunciation

1. In these sentences, the important stresses are <u>underlined</u>.

 Listen to cassette 1D.1 and repeat to practise.

    a. <u>Good</u> <u>mor</u>ning. <u>Good</u> after<u>noon</u>. <u>Good</u> <u>eve</u>ning.

    b. Can I <u>help</u> you?

    c. ex<u>pec</u>ting
       ex<u>pec</u>ting you?
       <u>What</u> <u>time</u> is she ex<u>pec</u>ting you?
       <u>What</u> <u>time</u> is he ex<u>pec</u>ting you?

    d. ap<u>point</u>ment
       I've <u>got</u> an ap<u>point</u>ment
       I've <u>got</u> an ap<u>point</u>ment with <u>Mark</u> <u>Roberts</u>.
       I've <u>got</u> an ap<u>point</u>ment with <u>Jenny</u> <u>Saunders</u>.

    e. <u>left</u>.
       on the <u>left</u>.
       It's the <u>first</u> <u>door</u> on the <u>left</u>.

2. *It's the <u>first</u> <u>door</u> on the <u>left</u>.*
    Make similar sentences for these directions.

    a. first/right

    b. second/left

    c. third/left

    d. third/right

 Listen to cassette 1D.2 and repeat to practise.

Check your answers in the key `1D.2`

 3. Listen to cassette 1D.3 and <u>underline</u> the important stresses in each sentence.

    a. Could I have your name, please? (three stresses)

    b. I'll see if he's free. (two stresses)

    c. Can you tell me where his office is? (three stresses)

    d. I'm afraid she's on the phone at the moment. (three stresses)

Check your answers in the key `1D.3`

 4. Rewind the cassette to the beginning of 1D.3.
    Listen and read aloud in time with the cassette.
    Practise until you can keep the same rhythm and speed as the cassette.

1E Speaking

I. Look at this floor plan.

Peter Knight	Alice Rowan	Carl Morris		Dominic Lowe	John Brown	Martin Shaw
Perry Lowden	Jean Wright	Kate Lynas	LIFT	Jean Fisher	Anne Taylor	Terry Bevan

Listen to cassette 1E.1.

You will hear six people asking for directions. Answer their questions from the floor plan. After you answer, you will hear an example answer.

Follow the model.

QUESTION	Can you tell me where John Brown's office is?
YOU	Come out of the lift, turn right and it's the second door on the left.
EXAMPLE	Come out of the lift, turn right and it's the second door on the left.

Check your answers in the key **1E.1**

2. A visitor arrives at reception.

Listen to cassette 1E.2 and read silently.

RECEPTIONIST	Good morning. Can I help you?
VISITOR	I've got an appointment with Mark Rogers.
RECEPTIONIST	What time is he expecting you?
VISITOR	Half past three.
RECEPTIONIST	Could I have your name, please?
VISITOR	John Smith.
RECEPTIONIST	Take a seat. I'll see if he's free.
VISITOR	Thank you.
RECEPTIONIST	I'm afraid he's in a meeting at the moment. Could you wait a few minutes?
VISITOR	Certainly.

3. Listen to cassette 1E.3.

This time you will hear only the receptionist. **You** are the visitor. Speak in the spaces and use your own name. Practise as many times as you want. Then close your book and practise again.

First conversations

Language for
asking and answering common questions
meeting people for the first time

2A Preparation

Most languages have expressions people use when they meet someone for the first time.

Match each expression on the left with the correct language on the right.

1. Lieto di fare sua conoscenza.   a. Hungarian
2. Encantado.   b. German
3. Örülök, hogy megismerheten.   c. Italian
4. Wie geht es Ihnen?   d. Portuguese
5. Enchanté.   e. Spanish
6. Muito prazer em conhocê-lo.   f. French

Check your answers in the key **2A**

What do you say in **your** language?

2B Listening

Carol Berkeley introduces Jean-Claude Duval to George Rotherford at a trade fair. They are meeting for the first time.

1. Before you listen, which of the expressions in the box do you think Jean-Claude and George will say to each other? Choose two.

> **How are you?**
> **How do you do?**
> **Hi!**
> **Pleased to meet you.**

Now listen to cassette 2B.1. Which expressions from the box did you hear?

Check your answers in the key **2B.1**

2. Listen to cassette 2B.2 and complete the table with George Rotherford's details.

	Jean-Claude Duval	**George Rotherford**
Nationality	French	a.
Job	Marketing Manager	b.
Company	Tekfarbe	c.
Location	New York	d.

Check your answers in the key **2B.2**

3. Listen to cassette 2B.3. Are these sentences True or False?
   a. Jean-Claude likes living in New York.
   b. George worked with Carol at Sony.
   c. George went to New York last month.

Check your answers in the key **2B.3**

2C Language check

1. Questions and answers

Match each question with the correct answer.

a. Where are you from? ——————
b. Where do you live?
c. What do you do?
d. Do you like Milan?
e. Who do you work for?
f. Where do you know Anne from?
g. Have you ever been to Italy?

i.   Hewlett-Packard.
ii. Yes, I have.
iii. Yes, I do.
iv. I'm an engineer.
v.   Milan, at the moment.
vi. We worked together at Microsoft.
vii. Holland, originally.

Now listen to cassette 2C.1.

Check your answers in the key **2C.1**

2. And you?

Listen to cassette 2C.2. What are **your** answers to these questions?
   a. Where are you from?
   b. Where do you live?
   c. What do you do?
   d. Who do you work for?

3. *Have you ever been to the USA?*

This is a useful question in conversations – especially between people from different countries.

It is a general question about the past. We use this question when we have no date, day, year or other reference to time. In this question *ever* means **at any time**.

When we talk about a specific time, we use the past simple, for example: Did you go to New York **last year**?

Question	Answers
Have you ever been to (the USA)?	→ Yes, I have. I went to (New York) (two years ago).
	→ No, I haven't.

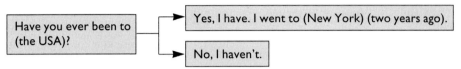

Complete this conversation. You will need to use more than one word in each space.

A Where do you live?

B In Montreal. .... Canada?

A Yes, ... I .... Quebec on business last year.

.... Quebec?

B No, ...

Now listen to cassette 2C.3.

Check your answers in the key **2C.3**

4. And you?

What are **your** answers to these questions?

a. Have you ever been to Great Britain or Ireland?
b. Have you ever been to the USA or Canada?
c. Have you ever been to Australia or New Zealand?

} If so, when did you go?

5. *Where are you from?*

In English, questions can end with prepositions.

Where do you know Anne from?

Make similar questions about these three people.

a. Peter
b. Abdul
c. Hans

Now listen to cassette 2C.5.

Check your answers in the key **2C.5**

6. And you?

Think of three people **you** know. Where do you know them from?

Compare your answers with the key **2C.6**

2D Pronunciation

1. In these sentences, the important stresses are <u>underlined</u>.

   Listen to cassette 2D.1 and repeat to practise.
   a. <u>do</u>?
      do you <u>do</u>?
      <u>How</u> do you <u>do</u>?
   b. <u>meet</u>
      to <u>meet</u> you.
      <u>Pleased</u> to <u>meet</u> you.
   c. New <u>York</u>?
      Do you <u>like</u> New <u>York</u>?
   d. <u>Japan</u>?
      <u>been</u> to <u>Japan</u>?
      Have you <u>ever</u> <u>been</u> to <u>Japan</u>?

2. Do you <u>like</u> New <u>York</u>?

   Make similar questions about these towns:
   a. <u>Paris</u>
   b. <u>London</u>
   c. <u>Tokyo</u>

   Listen to cassette 2D.2 and repeat to practise.

   Check your answers in the key `2D.2`

3. *Have you ever been to <u>Japan</u>?*

   Make similar questions about these countries.
   a. <u>Great</u> <u>Britain</u>
   b. the <u>USA</u>
   c. <u>Australia</u>

   Listen to cassette 2D.3 and repeat to practise.

   Check your answers in the key `2D.3`

4. Listen to cassette 2D.4 and <u>underline</u> the important stresses in each question.
   a. Where are you from? (two stresses)
   b. Where do you live? (two stresses)
   c. What do you do? (two stresses)
   d. Who do you work for? (three stresses)
   e. Where do you know Anne from? (four stresses)

   Check your answers in the key `2D.4`

5. Rewind the cassette to the beginning of 2D.4.

   Listen and read aloud in time with the cassette.

   Practise until you can keep the same rhythm and speed as the cassette.

2E Speaking

I. Carol Berkeley has just introduced John Hyde to George Rotherford at a party. Listen to cassette 2E.1 and read silently.

GEORGE ROTHERFORD	I'm sorry I didn't catch your name. You're … ?
JOHN HYDE	Hyde, John Hyde.
GEORGE ROTHERFORD	How do you do?
JOHN HYDE	Pleased to meet you.
GEORGE ROTHERFORD	Where are you from?
JOHN HYDE	The USA.
GEORGE ROTHERFORD	Ah. And where do you live?
JOHN HYDE	I'm from Ohio, but I live in Washington.
GEORGE ROTHERFORD	That's a place I've always wanted to visit. Do you like it there?
JOHN HYDE	Yes, I do.
GEORGE ROTHERFORD	What do you do?
JOHN HYDE	I'm a consultant.
GEORGE ROTHERFORD	Really? Who do you work for?
JOHN HYDE	Bennet and Ross.
GEORGE ROTHERFORD	A very good company. I'm with Panasonic in Canada.
JOHN HYDE	Really?
GEORGE ROTHERFORD	Have you ever been to Canada?
JOHN HYDE	No, I haven't.
GEORGE ROTHERFORD	Where do you know Carol from?
JOHN HYDE	We went to university together.
GEORGE ROTHERFORD	Ah.

2. Listen to cassette 2E.2.

This time you will hear only George Rotherford. **You** are the other person. Speak in the spaces and use real information about yourself. Practise as many times as you want. Then close your book and practise again.

Names and numbers

Language for

exchanging names and addresses, phone and fax numbers by telephone
asking people to repeat information
asking people to speak more slowly

3A Preparation

There are some differences between speaking to a person face-to-face and speaking to a person on the telephone.

For example, on the telephone:

You can't write things and show them to the other person.

You can't see the other person's face.

You cannot use diagrams or charts.

There are special expressions which we only use on the phone.

You can't see, or use, gestures.

The two people speaking are in different places.

The quality of sound is often bad.

Conversations are sometimes interrupted by technical problems.

Which do you think are the most serious difficulties? Choose three.

3B Listening

1. You will hear four telephone conversations. In each conversation, someone gives a name and spells it.

   The four names are in the box, but the letters are in the wrong order.

   Listen to cassette 3B.1 and write the names correctly.

   Play the conversations as many times as you want.

   > a. revaix treecibruaa
   > b. quodimien huegganir
   > c. darsna tetayef
   > d. nain wrotufna

   Check your answers in the key **3B.1**

2. You will hear three telephone conversations. In each conversation, someone asks for a telephone number.

Listen to cassette 3B.2 and write the three numbers.

Check your answers in the key **3B.2**

3. You will hear two telephone conversations.

Listen to cassette 3B.3 and complete the two record cards.

Play the conversations as many times as you want.

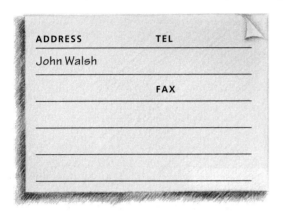

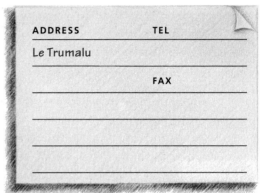

Check your answers in the key **3B.3**

3C *Language check*

1. **Questions 1**

Here are nine useful questions. Put the words in the correct order.

Follow the example.

please / you / again / that / could / say? Could you say that again, please?

a. could/name/give/me/you/your?
b. that/could/spell/you?
c. little/speak/more/could/you/slowly/a?
d. could/you/me/your/address/give?
e. number/your/phone/give/could/me/you?
f. I'm/you/say/sorry/did/what?
g. fax/what's/number/your?
h. six/seven/say/or/did/you/sorry/I'm?
i. sorry/a/little/could/speak/up/you/I'm?

Now listen to cassette 3C.1.

Check your answers in the key **3C.1**

2. **Questions 2**

In this telephone conversation, the language the receptionist uses is not appropriate. Use the questions from 3C.1 to make the conversation more polite and professional.

RECEPTIONIST	Who are you?
CALLER	George Smith.
RECEPTIONIST	What?
CALLER	GEORGE SMITH.
RECEPTIONIST	Spell it.
CALLER	S–M–I–T–H.
RECEPTIONIST	Tell me your phone number.
CALLER	4398 4532.
RECEPTIONIST	Slower!
CALLER	4398 4532.
RECEPTIONIST	Address?
CALLER	6, rue St Lazare, 75011 Paris.
RECEPTIONIST	What? Six or seven?
CALLER	Six.
RECEPTIONIST	Louder!
CALLER	SIX.
RECEPTIONIST	Fax?
CALLER	4398 2188.

Now listen to cassette 3C.2.

Check your answers in the key 3C.2

3D Pronunciation

. . . .

1. In these questions, the important stresses are <u>underlined</u>.

Listen to cassette 3D.1 and repeat to practise.

a. <u>name</u>?
<u>give</u> me your <u>name</u>?
Could you <u>give</u> me your <u>name</u>?

b. <u>seven</u>?
<u>six</u> or <u>seven</u>?
Did you <u>say</u> <u>six</u> or <u>seven</u>?

2. *Could you give me your <u>name</u>?*

Make similar sentences with these words.

a. ad<u>dress</u>
b. <u>phone</u> <u>number</u>
c. <u>fax</u> <u>number</u>

Listen to cassette 3D.2 and repeat to practise.

Check your answers in the key 3D.2

3. *Did you say <u>six</u> or <u>seven</u>?*

Make similar sentences with these numbers.
a. 4/5   b. 5/9   c. 9/1

Listen to cassette 3D.3 and repeat to practise.

Check your answers in the key 3D.3

4. In English, we use a special down-up (↘ ↗) intonation when we ask somebody to repeat something.

Listen to cassette 3D.4 and repeat to practise.

a. say?

What did you say?   I'm sorry, what did you say?

b. I'm sorry, what name did you say?

c. I'm sorry, what was the number?

d. I'm sorry, what was the address?

5. Listen to cassette 3D.5 and underline the important stresses in each question.

a. Could you speak more slowly?

b. Could you speak up a little?

c. Could you spell that?

Check your answers in the key 3D.5

6. Rewind the cassette to the beginning of 3D.5.

Listen and read aloud in time with the cassette.

Practise until you can keep the same rhythm and speed as the cassette.

7. Listen to cassette 3D.7 and read silently.

230 4567	two three oh, four five six seven
355 1809	three double five, one eight zero nine
476 3331	four seven six, treble three one

Note: **0** in British English is usually *oh*, but *zero* in American English.

8. Say these phone numbers.

a. 671 9352   c. 390 2299   e. 715 6661

b. 404 8766   d. 230 5113   f. 235 5988

Check your answers in the key 3D.8

Listen to cassette 3D.8 and repeat to practise.

9. On the telephone, we often need to spell names and addresses to be sure they are correct.

Look at the pronunciation guide and say the alphabet.

A /eɪ/   D /diː/   G /dʒiː/   J /dʒeɪ/   M /em/   P /piː/   S /es/   V /viː/   Y /waɪ/
B /biː/   E /iː/   H /eɪtʃ/   K /keɪ/   N /en/   Q /kjuː/   T /tiː/   W /ˈdʌbljuː/   Z /zed/(UK)
C /siː/   F /ef/   I /ʊɪ/   L /el/   O /əʊ/   R /ɑː/   U /juː/   X /eks/   /ziː/(US)

Listen to cassette 3D.9 and repeat to practise.

10. These eight cities contain all the letters of the alphabet. Say them and spell them.

BEIJING   GUADALAJARA   POZNAN   YOKOHAMA
NAXOS   WANAMIE   QUIOTEPEC   FULTONVILLE

Listen to cassette 3D.10 and repeat to practise.

3E Speaking

....

I. Look at this contact list.

	Tel	Fax
Q and A Software	760 5433	760 8722
Santini Distribution	981 0232	981 4466
Royal Crest Insurance	688 8099	688 2371
Cross Office Cleaning	465 9131	465 0019

Listen to cassette 3E.1.

You will hear eight questions. Answer the questions from the contact list. After you answer, you will hear an example answer.

Follow the model.

QUESTION	What's the phone number for Q and A Software?
YOU	seven six oh, five four double three
EXAMPLE	seven six oh, five four double three

2. English people often spell these words wrongly.

committee   professional   parallel   rhythm   personnel

Listen to cassette 3E.2.

You will hear five questions. Answer the questions. After you answer, you will hear an example answer.

Follow the model.

QUESTION	How do you spell committee?
YOU	C-O-double M-I-double T-double E
EXAMPLE	C-O-double M-I-double T-double E

3. Practise answering the questions in the box until you can give your name, the name and address of your company and your phone and fax numbers fluently.

Could you give me your name?	Could you give me the name of your company?
I'm sorry, what did you say?	Could you spell that?
Could you spell that?	Could you give me the address?
What's your phone number?	What's your fax number?

Listen to cassette 3E.3.

You will hear the same questions. Answer the questions.

Speak in the spaces. Practise as many times as you want. Then close your book and practise again.

Telephone messages

Language for

taking and leaving telephone messages

4A Preparation

 Read these telephone messages and put them in order.

a.

Message for: Giles St John
From: Alicia Lopez

The sales meeting's been postponed. They're looking for a date in August. She'll ring you.

☐

b.

Message for: Giles St John
From: Alicia Lopez

The sales meeting will be on 6th July at 10.30 in the Bowlan St offices. Ring if there are any problems. Tel: 349 3312.

☐

c.

MESSAGE FOR: *Alicia Lopez*
FROM: *Giles St John*

Please call asap about the sales meeting: he needs to know the time and date.
Tel: 234 5780.

1

d.

MESSAGE FOR: *Alicia Lopez*
FROM: *Giles St John*

Re: sales meeting – 6th is impossible. Please ring him before 5 p.m. today.
Tel: 234 5780.

☐

Check your answers in the key **4A**

4B Listening

1. Lindy Cohen works for Crossways, a shipping company. She is out of the office when John Collis rings from Munich so he leaves a message with her secretary.

The secretary makes two mistakes in the message.

▣ Read the message. Then listen to cassette 4B.1 and find the mistakes.

Date: 16th July   **Time:** 10.30 a.m.
Message for: Lindy Cohen   **From:** John Collis

Re: next week's visit to Germany – Mr Collis says that 10 a.m. is a difficult time for the marketing meeting on the first day. Can you change it to 11 a.m.? Please ring back this afternoon before 6 p.m. to confirm. Tel: Munich 43 82 45.

Check your answers in the key **4B.1**

2. Greta Hass rang Lindy Cohen at home and left a message on her answering machine.

▣ Listen to cassette 4B.2 and complete this note for Lindy.

Greta rang. She'd like to meet for ....

next week on .... Call her any evening

after .... Tel: ....

Check your answers in the key **4B.2**

3. Someone rang Crossways when the office was closed and left a message for Lindy Cohen on the answering machine.

▣ Listen to cassette 4B.3 and write a message for Lindy.

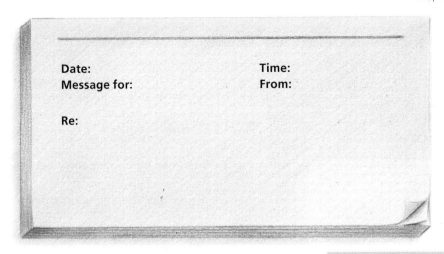

Date: **Time:**
Message for: **From:**

Re:

Check your answers in the key **4B.3**

4C Language check

1. A conversation

Put these sentences in the right order to make a telephone conversation.

Receptionist

☐ Goodbye.

☐ And your number?

☐ One moment … I'm afraid he's in a meeting. Can I take a message?

☐ How do you spell that?

☐ Hawker Robins. Good morning. Can I help you?

☐ Certainly. Could I have your name, please?

☐ I'll see that he gets your message.

Caller

☐ L-E-B L-I Q-U-E.

☐ Thank you very much. Goodbye.

☐ Could I speak to Phil Allison, please?

☐ Yes. Could you ask him to call me before four o'clock? I'm ringing about the AJK proposal.

☐ John Leblique.

☐ 453 2121.

Now listen to cassette 4C.1.

Check your answers in the key **4C.1**

2. A message

Complete this answering machine message with words from the list.

> I'm ringing about   could he call me   this is   I'd like to speak to   my number's

.... Mark Levy of AGC. .... John Benson.

.... the marketing meeting. .... as

soon as possible? .... 756 8343. Thanks.

Note: *This is Mark Levy of AGC.* When you give your name on the telephone, say *This is …* not *I am …* and give your full name.

Now listen to cassette 4C.2.

Check your answers in the key **4C.2**

📖 **3. *Could you ask him to call me later?***

Look at the plan. Notice the use of the infinitive (**to** + verb).

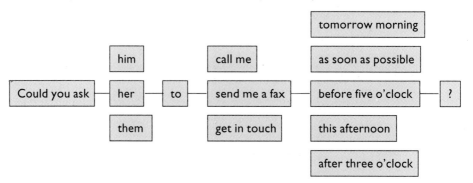

Read these situations and use the plan to make a question for each one.

a. You phone your lawyer in London but she is in a meeting. You speak to her assistant. You're going out but you'll be back at three o'clock.

b. You phone a client but he's out. You speak to his secretary. You're leaving the office at five o'clock.

c. You phone the manager of your New York office but he's out for the day. You speak to his personal assistant.

d. There is a crisis in the Finance Department. You ring the Financial Director, who is on holiday, but she is not in her hotel. You speak to the hotel receptionist.

▦ Now listen to cassette 4C.3.

Check your answers in the key **4C.3**

4D *Pronunciation*

I. In these sentences, the important stresses are <u>underlined</u>.

▦ Listen to cassette 4D.I and repeat to practise.

a. <u>Brown</u>?
   Mr <u>Brown</u>?
   <u>speak</u> to Mr <u>Brown</u>?
   Could I <u>speak</u> to Mr <u>Brown</u>?
   Could I <u>speak</u> to Mr <u>Brown</u>, please?
   Could I <u>speak</u> to Ms <u>White</u>, please?

b. <u>out</u>.
   He's <u>out</u>.
   I'm a<u>fraid</u> he's <u>out</u>.
   I'm a<u>fraid</u> she's <u>out</u>.
   I'm a<u>fraid</u> he's in a <u>meet</u>ing.
   I'm a<u>fraid</u> she's on another <u>line</u>.

c. <u>sales</u> <u>meet</u>ing.
   the <u>sales</u> <u>meet</u>ing.
   I'm <u>ring</u>ing about the <u>sales</u> <u>meet</u>ing.

2. *I'm <u>ring</u>ing about the <u>sales</u> <u>meet</u>ing.*

Make similar sentences about these meetings.

a.   pro<u>duc</u>tion

b.   a<u>ccounts</u>

c.   <u>mar</u>keting

Listen to cassette 4D.2 and repeat to practise.

Check your answers in the key **4D.2**

3.   Listen and <u>underline</u> the important stresses in each sentence.

a.   Can I take a message? (two stresses)

b.   I'll tell him you called. (two stresses)

c.   Could you ask her to call me? (two stresses)

Check your answers in the key **4D.3**

4.   Rewind the cassette to the beginning of 4D.3.

Listen and read aloud in time with the cassette.

Practise until you can keep the same rhythm and speed as the cassette.

4E Speaking

I.   Lana Corning of Wise Electronics wrote this list.

Things to do ...

✦ **Call Gordon Klein of Q and A Software about our new**

accounting system.

✦ **Talk to Annie Pastori of Santini about a late delivery**

(order no. 23212).

✦ **Call Kenji Hata of the Sumiti Bank about land**

investments in the Far East.

You are Lana Corning. You make the three phone calls but you get an answering machine each time.

Listen to cassette 4E.1. Leave an appropriate message on each answering machine. Speak after the tone.

After you leave each message, you will hear an example message.

2. Look at this conversation plan.

Receptionist

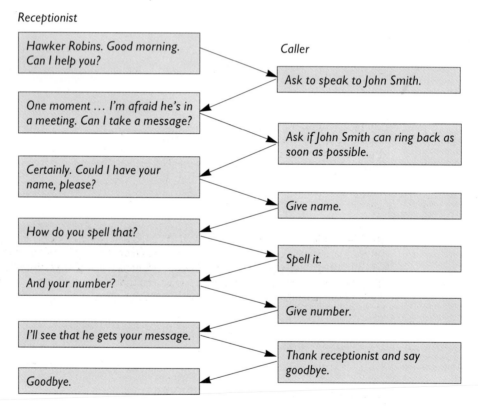

Receptionist	Caller
Hawker Robins. Good morning. Can I help you?	
	Ask to speak to John Smith.
One moment ... I'm afraid he's in a meeting. Can I take a message?	
	Ask if John Smith can ring back as soon as possible.
Certainly. Could I have your name, please?	
	Give name.
How do you spell that?	
	Spell it.
And your number?	
	Give number.
I'll see that he gets your message.	
	Thank receptionist and say goodbye.
Goodbye.	

Listen to cassette 4E.2.

You will hear only the receptionist. **You** are the caller.

Follow the conversation plan and speak in the spaces.

Practise as many times as you want. Then close your book and practise again.

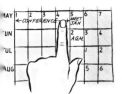

UNIT 5

Schedules

Language for

understanding and saying dates
asking and answering questions about schedules

5A Preparation

You will hear Jill Warburton, a director of a British publishing company, talking about this schedule.

Annual General Meeting:	6th–8th June
Regional Sales Meeting:	14th June
Budapest Book Fair:	2nd–6th July
Marketing Meeting (Paris):	21st July

Listen to cassette 5A and read silently.

■ *Can you tell us about your schedule for the next couple of months, Jill?*
Well, there's the annual general meeting, that's from the sixth to the eighth of June. The regional sales meeting's on the fourteenth of June, and, let me see, the Budapest Book Fair is the first week of July, from the second to the sixth. On the twenty-first of July, there's a marketing meeting in Paris and … that's it.

5B Listening

I. Listen to cassette 5B.1.

You will hear three people asking about these meetings. Which meeting is on which date?

Meetings	Dates
a. Marketing Meeting	i. 1st June
b. Sales Meeting	ii. 5th March
c. Annual Conference	iii. 3rd May

Check your answers in the key **5B.1**

■ 27

2. Rewind the cassette to the beginning of 5B.1.

Listen again and put the words of these questions in the correct order.

a. marketing/the/when's/meeting?

b. date/meeting/of/what's/the/sales/the?

c. for/when's/scheduled/conference/the?

Check your answers in the key **5B.1**

3. In the New Products Division at Q and A Software, Peter Dressler (Head of New Products), Janet Shields (Head of Marketing) and Marc de la Tour (Marketing Executive) are meeting to decide who is going to these trade fairs.

Fair	Dates	Representative(s)
a. Expotec, Casablanca	2nd–7th October	Janet Shields
b. Frankfurt Technology Fair		
c. ComInTech, Geneva		
d. Sydney AI Fair		
e. InfoTek, San Francisco		

Listen to cassette 5B.3 and complete the table.

Concentrate **only** on the information you need.

Play the cassette as many times as you want.

Check your answers in the key **5B.3**

5C Language check

I. Prepositions

Complete these sentences with the correct prepositions from the list.

on	to	of	from

a. Expotec starts .... the second .... October and finishes .... the seventh.

b. The Sydney AI Fair is .... the eighteenth .... the twenty-third .... September.

c. ComInTech is .... July; .... the sixth .... the tenth.

Now listen to cassette 5C.1.

Check your answers in the key **5C.1**

2. The future with the present simple

You can use the present simple to talk about the future when you are talking about organised events.

When's the marketing meeting? What's the date of the marketing meeting? When's the marketing meeting scheduled for?	It's on the third of May. It's from the third to the fifth of May.

Now make similar questions and answers about these events.

a. Sales Meeting: 6th December

b. Press Conference: 9th June

c. Production Meeting: 21st April

d. Conference: 1st–5th February

 Now listen to cassette 5C.2.

 Check your answers in the key **5C.2**

5D Pronunciation

1. When we say dates in English we do not say *one, two, three*; we say *first, second, third*. Look at the box and say the dates and months.

1st first	13th thirteenth	25th twenty-fifth	January
2nd second	14th fourteenth	26th twenty-sixth	February
3rd third	15th fifteenth	27th twenty-seventh	March
4th fourth	16th sixteenth	28th twenty-eighth	April
5th fifth	17th seventeenth	29th twenty-ninth	May
6th sixth	18th eighteenth	30th thirtieth	June
7th seventh	19th nineteenth	31st thirty-first	July
8th eighth	20th twentieth		August
9th ninth	21st twenty-first		September
10th tenth	22nd twenty-second		October
11th eleventh	23rd twenty-third		November
12th twelfth	24th twenty-fourth		December

Listen to cassette 5D.1 and repeat to practise.

2. Listen to cassette 5D.2 and read silently.

1/12 the first of December   2/11 the second of November   3/10 the third of October

Note: In British English **1/12** is *the first of December*; in American English **1/12** is *the twelfth of January*.

3. Say these dates.

a. 4/9	d. 7/6	g. 10/3
b. 5/8	e. 8/5	h. 11/2
c. 6/7	f. 9/4	i. 12/1

Listen to cassette 5D.3 and repeat to practise.

Check your answers in the key **5D.3**

4. *The marketing meeting is on the eleventh of January.*

Look at the schedule and make similar sentences about these events.

a. 22/6: Production Meeting
b. 5/2: Sales Meeting
c. 5/7: Finance Meeting
d. 25/4–3/5: Paris Trade Fair
e. 31/9–4/10: Annual Conference

Listen to cassette 5D.4 and repeat to practise.

Check your answers in the key **5D.4**

5. Listen to cassette 5D.5 and <u>underline</u> the important stresses in each question.

a. When's the marketing meeting? (three stresses)
b. What's the date of the sales meeting? (four stresses)
c. When's the conference scheduled for? (four stresses)

Check your answers in the key **5D.5**

6. Rewind the cassette to the beginning of 5D.5.

Listen and read aloud in time with the cassette.

Practise until you can keep the same rhythm and speed as the cassette.

7. Listen to cassette 5D.7.

You will hear five questions. Answer the questions.

Speak in the spaces and repeat to practise.

5E Speaking

1. Look at this schedule of meetings and events.

Q and A Software

Schedule of meetings and events

Stuttgart Tech Fair	3/12–5/12
Regional Sales Meeting	14/12
Annual Conference	12/1–16/1
Newport Communications Fair	21/1–23/1
Launch of Fotoscan in Europe	31/1
Launch of Fotoscan in Japan	12/2
Annual Inspection Visit	15/4–18/4

Listen to cassette 5E.1.

You will hear seven questions. Answer the questions from the schedule. After you answer, you will hear an example answer.

Follow the model.

QUESTION	When's the Stuttgart Tech Fair?
YOU	It's from the third to the fifth of December.
EXAMPLE	It's from the third to the fifth of December.

2. What's on **your** schedule?

Make a list of events you and/or your company are planning and use the language in the box to talk about them.

The .... is on the .... of ....
The .... is from the .... of .... to the .... of ....

Date	Event

Sales figures

Language for
talking about figures changing through time

6A Preparation

Talk about these sales graphs in your own language.

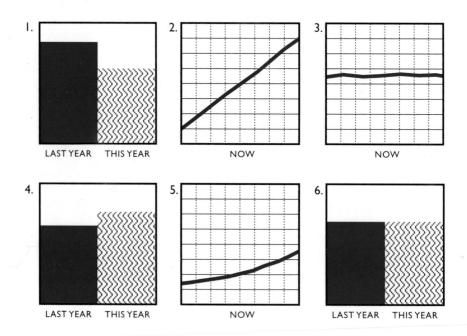

1. LAST YEAR   THIS YEAR

2. NOW

3. NOW

4. LAST YEAR   THIS YEAR

5. NOW

6. LAST YEAR   THIS YEAR

6B Listening

I. You will hear the beginning of a meeting at McKillin, a soft drinks manufacturer.

There are seven people in the meeting: Jenny Dewan, Marketing Manager for Western Europe, and the regional sales managers for the six areas in the box.

> France   Spain and Portugal   UK and Ireland   Italy   Germany   Greece

Listen to cassette 6B.1.

You will hear each regional manager talking about sales in his or her area. Which of the graphs in 6A show the sales in each region?

Check your answers in the key **6B.1**

Now listen to cassette 6B.1 again and complete these sentences. Write one word in each space.

FRANCE Not bad. We're .... last year.

SPAIN AND
PORTUGAL Well, we didn't start the year very well, but sales are .... very

.... now.

UK AND IRELAND About .... as last year.

ITALY Not very good, really. We're .... last year.

GERMANY We've had a good year. At the moment sales are ....

GREECE Well, we're very new in Greece, so sales levels are quite low. But, sales are ....

.... I feel optimistic.

Check your answers in the key **6B.1**

2. Look at the graph.

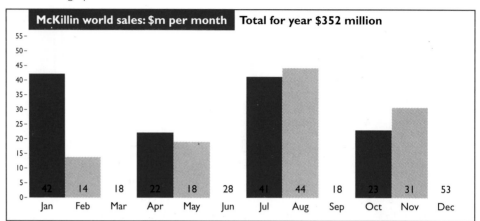

You will hear Jenny Dewan speaking about McKillin's world sales for this financial year.

Listen to cassette 6B.2 and answer these questions.

a. What were the company's total sales last year?

b. What were last year's figures for:
   i. March?   iii. August?
   ii. May?   iv. December?

Check your answers in the key **6B.2**

6C Language check

I. Vocabulary

Listen to cassette 6C.1 and read silently.

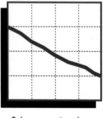

Sales are going down slowly.

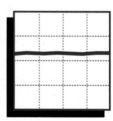

Sales are holding steady.

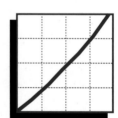

Sales are going up rapidly.

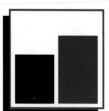

Sales are $1m (or 33%) up on last year.

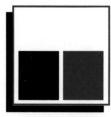

Sales are about the same as last year.

Sales are $1m (or 33%) down on last year.

2. What's happening?

Look at these sales figures for the first quarter of the year and say what is happening in each region.

Follow the example.

In France, sales are going up rapidly.

Sales figures by region: $US			
Region	**January**	**February**	**March**
France	2,500,000	3,251,000	4,311,000
Spain	2,210,000	2,212,000	2,216,000
Germany	4,400,000	3,675,000	3,108,000
Italy	3,221,000	3,220,000	3,221,000
Japan	2,849,000	2,701,000	2,695,000

 Now listen to cassette 6C.2.

Check your answers in the key **6C.2**

3. This year/Last year

Look at the sales figures for March for last year and this year. Talk about the situation in each region.

Follow the examples.

In France, sales are $410,000 up on last year.
In France, sales are 11 per cent up on last year.

Sales figures by region: $US				
March: this year/last year				
Region	**last year**	**this year**	**variation**	**%**
France	3,901,000	4,311,000	410,000	11
Spain	2,490,000	2,219,000	-271,000	-12
Germany	3,002,000	3,108,000	106,000	4
Italy	3,450,000	3,221,000	-229,000	-7
Japan	2,694,000	2,695,000	1,000	0

 Now listen to cassette 6C.3.

Check your answers in the key **6C.3**

6D Pronunciation

∙∙

1. Say these figures.

> 9   89   789   6,789   56,789   456,789   3,456,789   23,456,789   123,456,789
> $2^1/_2$ million   2.5m   2,500,000   33%   10%   5%

Listen to cassette 6D.1 and repeat to practise.

2. In these sentences, the important stresses are <u>underlined</u>.

Listen to cassette 6D.2 and repeat to practise.

a. <u>down</u>
<u>Sales</u> are <u>down</u>
<u>Sales</u> are <u>down</u> on <u>last</u> <u>year</u>.
<u>Sales</u> are <u>two</u> <u>million</u> <u>down</u> on <u>last</u> <u>year</u>.
<u>Sales</u> are <u>five</u> per <u>cent</u> <u>down</u> on <u>last</u> <u>year</u>.

b. <u>up</u>
<u>Sales</u> are <u>up</u>
<u>Sales</u> are <u>up</u> on <u>last</u> <u>year</u>.
<u>Sales</u> are <u>three</u> <u>million</u> <u>up</u> on <u>last</u> <u>year</u>.
<u>Sales</u> are <u>eight</u> per <u>cent</u> <u>up</u> on <u>last</u> <u>year</u>.

c. <u>Sales</u> are <u>going</u> <u>down</u>.
<u>Sales</u> are <u>going</u> <u>down</u> <u>slowly</u>.
<u>Sales</u> are <u>going</u> <u>down</u> <u>rapidly</u>.

d. <u>Sales</u> are <u>going</u> <u>up</u>.
<u>Sales</u> are <u>going</u> <u>up</u> <u>slowly</u>.
<u>Sales</u> are <u>going</u> <u>up</u> <u>rapidly</u>.

3. Listen to cassette 6D.3 and <u>underline</u> the important stresses in each sentence.

a. <u>Sales</u> are about the <u>same</u> as <u>last</u> <u>year</u>. (four stresses)
b. <u>Sales</u> are <u>holding</u> <u>steady</u>. (three stresses)

Check your answers in the key 6D.3

4. Rewind the cassette to the beginning of 6D.3.

Listen and read aloud in time with the cassette.

Practise until you can keep the same rhythm and speed as the cassette.

6E *Speaking*

I. Look at the sales chart.

Whittle and Kohning

Sales figures by region Oct–Dec ($US) + comparison with last year

Region	October	November	December	Total Oct–Dec	Total Oct–Dec last year	% variation
Denmark	790,000	853,000	1,050,000	2,693,000	2,421,000	11
Norway	1,012,000	992,000	901,000	2,905,000	3,150,000	-8
Finland	1,040,000	1,105,000	1,188,000	3,333,000	2,987,000	12
Sweden	1,849,000	1,841,000	1,848,000	5,538,000	5,543,000	0
Totals	4,691,000	4,791,000	4,987,000	14,469,000	14,101,000	3

You work for Whittle and Kohning, a pharmaceutical company, as Sales Director for Scandinavia. The Marketing Manager for Western Europe is going to ask you five questions.

Listen to cassette 6E.1 and answer the questions from the chart. After you answer, you will hear an example answer.

Follow the model.

QUESTION	What's the situation in Denmark?
YOU	Sales are going up rapidly and we're eleven per cent up on last year.
EXAMPLE	Sales are going up rapidly and we're eleven per cent up on last year.

2. What is happening now in your country?

Make some notes on each of these areas.
a. inflation
b. interest rates
c. house prices
d. unemployment

Now listen to cassette 6E.2.

You will hear four questions. Answer the questions.

Speak in the spaces and repeat to practise.

3. What is happening in your company?

Talk about sales in your department/company.

Making appointments

Language for

talking about appointments
making appointments

7A Preparation

John Waterman works for a company called Hearst Behring. You will hear him talking about his appointments for the week.

Listen to cassette 7A and look at his diary.

MONDAY	TUESDAY	WEDNESDAY	THURSDAY	FRIDAY
		11.00: Divisional Meeting		10.00: Christina Bunnenberg (CJK contract)
		12.30: lunch, Andrew Symes	1.00: lunch, Sue Bowlan	
	2.00: Etta Caducci (Unital)	2.30 Harlan Brown (MXS)		
	4.00: Royce Lowton (production figures)			

7B Listening

. . . .

I. You will hear four telephone conversations.

Conversation 1: Christina Bunnenberg calls John Waterman.

Conversation 2: John Waterman calls François Letellier.

Conversation 3: John Waterman calls Harlan Brown.

Conversation 4: Christina Bunnenberg calls John Waterman.

All the conversations happen on Tuesday morning.

Listen to cassette 7B.1 and make the necessary changes to John Waterman's diary in 7A.

Concentrate **only** on the information you need to correct the diary.

Play the conversations as many times as you want.

> *Check your answers in the key* **7B.1**

Now listen to cassette 7B.1 again and complete these sentences. Write one word in each space.

Conversation 1

CHRISTINA
BUNNENBERG Can .... tomorrow?

JOHN
WATERMAN I'm afraid I'm .... tomorrow. .... Thursday?

Conversation 2

JOHN
WATERMAN What are .... tomorrow morning at nine?

FRANÇOIS
LETELLIER Tomorrow morning is impossible, I'm afraid. .... in the afternoon?

Conversation 3

HARLAN
BROWN Oh, that's a pity. Can .... another time?

I'm .... Friday morning.

Conversation 4

> *Check your answers in the key* **7B.1**

CHRISTINA
BUNNENBERG Can .... to my office at about eleven?

JOHN
WATERMAN Eleven. Yes, fine. OK. .... tomorrow.

7C Language check

1. Prepositions

Here is Maria Salerno's diary for the week.

Monday	Tuesday	Wednesday	Thursday	Friday
12.30: lunch with Joe Gianelli	10.00: sales meeting	10.00: factory visit		8.00 flight to Paris (AF213)

Complete Maria's description of her appointments with the correct prepositions from the list. In three of the spaces no preposition is necessary.

on   in   at   to   with   for

a. .... today I'm having lunch .... Joe Gianelli.
b. .... tomorrow morning .... ten I'm going .... a sales meeting.
c. I'm visiting .... the factory .... Wednesday .... the morning.
d. .... 8 a.m. .... Friday I'm flying .... Paris .... a training course.

Now listen to cassette 7C.1.   **Check your answers in the key** **7C.1**

2. The future with the present continuous

In Maria's description of her appointments (7C.1), she is talking about the future but she uses the present continuous (**be** + verb + **-ing**).

You can use the present continuous to talk about the future when you are talking about personal plans.

Read these notes and make complete sentences using the present continuous.

Follow the example.

Monday/go/New York/a meeting   On Monday, I'm going to New York for a meeting.

a. Tomorrow/have/lunch/La Tour d'Or/a client
b. Wednesday/go/Budapest/a trade fair
c. stay/the Intercontinental/Wednesday night
d. Thursday/meet/Maria Csemi
e. Friday/fly/Mexico/a holiday

Now listen to cassette 7C.2.   **Check your answers in the key** **7C.2**

7D Pronunciation

1. Say the days of the week.

> <u>Mon</u>day   <u>Tues</u>day   <u>Wednes</u>day   <u>Thurs</u>day   <u>Fri</u>day   <u>Satur</u>day   <u>Sun</u>day

Note: **Wednesday** is pronounced with only two syllables: /ˈwenzdɪ/.

Listen to cassette 7D.1 and repeat to practise.

2. In these sentences, the most important stresses are <u>underlined</u>.

Listen to cassette 7D.2 and repeat to practise.

  a. <u>Mon</u>day <u>mor</u>ning?
   Are you <u>free</u> on <u>Mon</u>day <u>mor</u>ning?
   Are you <u>free</u> on <u>Tues</u>day after<u>noon</u>?
   Are you <u>free</u> on <u>Wednes</u>day at <u>ten</u>?

  b. <u>Tues</u>day after<u>noon</u>?
   <u>What</u> are you <u>do</u>ing on <u>Tues</u>day after<u>noon</u>?
   <u>What</u> are you <u>do</u>ing on <u>Fri</u>day <u>mor</u>ning?
   <u>What</u> are you <u>do</u>ing on <u>Satur</u>day at <u>three</u>?

  c. <u>Wednes</u>day at <u>one</u>?
   Can we <u>meet</u> on <u>Wednes</u>day at <u>one</u>?
   Can we <u>meet</u> on <u>Fri</u>day after<u>noon</u>?
   Can we <u>meet</u> on <u>Mon</u>day at <u>nine</u>?

  d. <u>Thurs</u>day at <u>three</u>?
   <u>How</u> about <u>Thurs</u>day at <u>three</u>?
   <u>How</u> about <u>Tues</u>day <u>mor</u>ning?
   <u>How</u> about <u>Sun</u>day after<u>noon</u>?

3. Listen to cassette 7D.3 and <u>underline</u> the important stresses in each sentence.
  a. I'm flying to New York on Monday. (three stresses)
  b. I'm having lunch with Mr Baker on Tuesday. (four stresses)
  c. I'm meeting Mr Helms on Wednesday. (three stresses)
  d. I'm afraid I'm busy on Thursday. (three stresses)
  e. I'm free on Friday morning. (three stresses)

Check your answers in the key **7D.3**

4. Rewind the cassette to the beginning of 7D.3.

Listen and read aloud in time with the cassette.

Practise until you can keep the same rhythm and speed as the cassette.

7E Speaking

1. Look at your diary for next week.

MONDAY	TUESDAY	WEDNESDAY	THURSDAY	FRIDAY
9.00: sales meeting	trade fair (all day)	8.30: return flight (KLM219)	10.00: visit factory	
		12.30: have lunch with Bill Canning		1.00: have lunch with Joanne (ICL)
3.00: BA433 to Amsterdam for trade fair			2.30: meeting at ICL	3.00: finish early

Listen to cassette 7E.1.

You will hear eight questions. Answer the questions from the diary. After you answer you will hear an example answer.

Follow the model.

QUESTION	What are you doing on Monday morning?
YOU	I'm going to a sales meeting.
EXAMPLE	I'm going to a sales meeting.

2. Listen to cassette 7E.2 and look at the diary in 7E.1.

John Waterman is fixing an appointment with a client.

3. Listen to cassette 7E.3.

This time you will hear only John Waterman. **You** are the client.

Follow the conversation plan and speak in the spaces. Use the diary in 7E.1.

Practise as many times as you want.

John Waterman

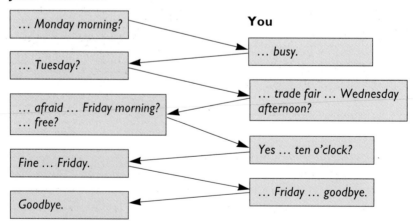

4. What appointments do **you** have next week?

Listen to cassette 7E.4.

You will hear eight questions. Answer the questions from **your** diary.

Prices and discounts

Language for

asking for information by telephone
talking about prices and discounts

8A Preparation

📖 **1.** Who do you agree with?

Experience is the most important thing for a manager, but formal training helps you to understand and use your experience.

You learn to be a manager through experience: formal training is not very important.

Experience and training are important, but there is no substitute for natural ability.

Management is complicated and formal training is absolutely essential.

2. Match each question with the correct answer.

a. What's the price?
b. What discount can you give me if I buy five?
c. What are the terms of payment?
d. How long is the guarantee?
e. Is there a special price for new customers?

i.   7.5 per cent
ii. twelve months
iii. no, there isn't
iv. thirty days
v.   £1,250

Check your answers in the key **8A.2**

8B Listening

1. Before you listen, read the advertisement and answer the questions.

Strategic Management in Global Markets A two-week course for senior managers *For more information, contact:* Executive Education Programs Château Marnier, 230 rue de la Ferme St Lazare, Nice Tel: 981 234 Fax 981 412	An intensive, practical course giving the senior manager a unique perspective on doing business in a global market. Seminars given by leaders of international organisations, with English as the language of instruction.

a. How long is the course?

b. Who is it for?

c. What language is the course in?

Check your answers in the key **8B.1**

2. Carol Parry is Human Resources Manager at Locke-Burnett, an engineering company. She phones Executive Education Programs to ask for more information about the course in the advertisement.

Listen to cassette 8B.2 and note the answers to Carol Parry's questions.

Concentrate **only** on the information you need to answer her questions.

Play the conversation as many times as you want.

EXECUTIVE EDUCATION PROGRAMS
STRATEGIC MANAGEMENT IN GLOBAL MARKETS Tel: Nice 981 234

Questions

a. Timetable?

b. Course content?

c. Price per participant? (VAT?)

d. Special price for companies?

e. Discount for three participants?

f. Terms of payment?

g. Arrangements for accommodation?

h. Dates of the next course?

i. Deadline for reservations?

Check your answers in the key **8B.2**

Now listen to cassette 8B.2 again and complete these questions. You will need to write more than one word in each space.

.... timetable of the course?

.... the content of the course?

.... the price per participant?

.... include VAT?

.... a price for company clients?

And if I send three people on the course, ... a discount?

.... your terms of payment?

.... accommodation? .... arrange that?

.... the dates of the next course?

.... still places?

.... deadline for reserving places?

Check your answers in the key **8B.2**

8C Language check

I. *I'd like some information about …*

This is a useful way to start a conversation when you want some information about something.

I'd like some information about *I'd like some information about*	+	NOUN *one of your courses.*

Make similar sentences with these two nouns.

a. your products
b. your services

Now listen to cassette 8C.1.

Check your answers in the key **8C.1**

2. **Discounts**

Use the sentences in the box to complete this conversation from 8B.2.

> a. If you send five, one place is free.
> b. If the participant's company is paying for the course, the price is $980.
> c. If you pay within ten days, there's a 3 per cent discount.
> d. If I send three people on the course, can you offer me a discount?

CAROL PARRY Do you have a price for company clients?

TOM ATKINSON Yes, we do. ....

CAROL PARRY And ....

TOM ATKINSON Not for three people, no. But ....

CAROL PARRY That's interesting. What are your terms of payment?

TOM ATKINSON Thirty days. ....

Check your answers in the key **8C.2**

■ 45

3. Conditions

Discount offers often depend on special conditions.

CONDITION (If ...)		OFFER
If the participant's company is paying for the course,	+	the price is $980.
If you send five,		one place is free.
If you pay within ten days,		there's a 3 per cent discount.

Read these notes and make a sentence with **If** about each one.

Follow the example.

Condition:	order before 12th April	If you order before 12th April, the price is £499.
Offer:	price £499	

a. Condition: pay within ten days
   Offer: 2.5 per cent discount

b. Condition: buy ten
   Offer: one free

c. Condition: pay cash
   Offer: price £150

d. Condition: spend $100 or more
   Offer: 6 per cent discount

Now listen to cassette 8C.3.

Check your answers in the key 8C.3

4. And you?

Write a sentence about a discount which your company offers.

5. *Can you tell me the price?*

We use *Can you tell me ... ?* to make a question more polite.

Make polite questions for these answers.

Follow the example.

£175	Can you tell me the price?

a. John Smith

b. 8.30 p.m.

c. 16th August

d. 357 6512

e. 198, Warrington Road

Now listen to cassette 8C.5.

Check your answers in the key 8C.5

6. *Does that include VAT?*

Make similar questions about these costs.

a. service   b. transport

Now listen to cassette 8C.6.

Check your answers in the key 8C.6

7. Asking the price

There are many ways to ask the price in English.

Look at these questions. One of them is not correct. Which one?

a. How much is it?

b. How much is the price?

c. How much does it cost?

d. Can you tell me the price?

e. What's the price?

Check your answers in the key 8C.7

8D Pronunciation

. . . .

1. All these numbers are in the unit. Listen to cassette 8D.1 and repeat to practise.

a. 7.5%	g. 2.5%
b. 12 months	h. £150
c. 30 days	i. 6%
d. £1,250	j. 357 6512
e. $980	k. 8.30 p.m.
f. 12th April	l. 16th August

2. In these sentences, the important stresses are <u>underlined</u>.

Listen to cassette 8D.2 and repeat to practise.

a. infor<u>ma</u>tion

   I'd <u>like</u> some infor<u>ma</u>tion

   I'd <u>like</u> some infor<u>ma</u>tion about your <u>pro</u>ducts.

   I'd <u>like</u> some infor<u>ma</u>tion about your <u>ser</u>vices.

b. <u>tell</u> me

   Can you <u>tell</u> me

   Can you <u>tell</u> me the <u>price</u>?

   Can you <u>tell</u> me the <u>date</u>?

   Can you <u>tell</u> me the <u>time</u>?

c. Does that inc<u>lude</u> VA<u>T</u>?

   Does that inc<u>lude</u> <u>ser</u>vice?

   Does that inc<u>lude</u> <u>trans</u>port?

3. Listen to cassette 8D.3 and <u>underline</u> the important stresses in each question.

a. How much does it cost? (three stresses)

b. What's the price? (two stresses)

c. Do you have a price for company clients? (four stresses)

d. What are your terms of payment? (three stresses)

Check your answers in the key 8D.2

4. Rewind the cassette to the beginning of 8D.3.

Listen and read aloud in time with the cassette.

Practise until you can keep the same rhythm and speed as the cassette.

8E Speaking

1. Look at Q and A Software's price/discount list for Pro-Word.

Q and A Software
PRO-WORD

Standard price (ex VAT):	$530
Price for company clients:	$499
Discount on 10 or more:	10%
Discount for early payment:	2.5%*

* for payment within 15 days

 Listen to cassette 8E.1.

You will hear four questions. Answer the questions from the list. After you answer you will hear an example answer.

Follow the model.

QUESTION	Can you tell me the price?
YOU	It's five hundred and thirty dollars.
EXAMPLE	It's five hundred and thirty dollars.

2. Listen to cassette 8E.2.

A customer is phoning Q and A Software to ask about prices.

3. Listen to cassette 8E.3.

This time you will hear only the receptionist and sales representative. **You** are the customer.

Follow the conversation plan and speak in the spaces.

Practise as many times as you want.

Q and A Software

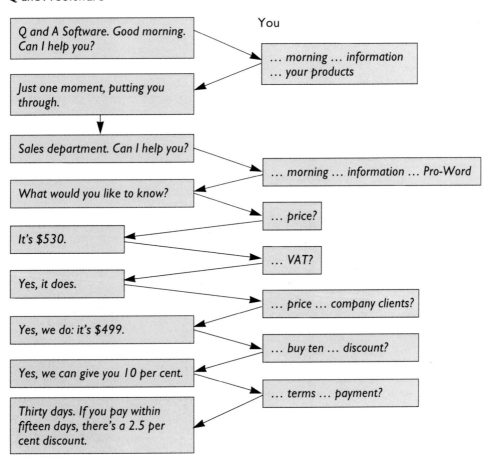

You

Q and A Software. Good morning. Can I help you?

... morning ... information ... your products

Just one moment, putting you through.

Sales department. Can I help you?

... morning ... information ... Pro-Word

What would you like to know?

... price?

It's $530.

... VAT?

Yes, it does.

... price ... company clients?

Yes, we do: it's $499.

... buy ten ... discount?

Yes, we can give you 10 per cent.

... terms ... payment?

Thirty days. If you pay within fifteen days, there's a 2.5 per cent discount.

Company profiles

Language for

giving and understanding short descriptions of companies
asking and answering questions about companies

9A Preparation

1. How much do you know about your company? Answer these questions.
   a. Where is the head office of your company?
   b. How many people work for your company?
   c. How much money did your company make last year?
   d. How much is your company worth?

2. Write these words in your own language. Then choose the correct word to complete each sentence.

turnover	
based	
employees	
value	
profits	

   a. The company is .... in Seville.
   b. They paid 10 per cent above the market ....
   c. Our .... last year was $196 million.
   d. Last year we made pre-tax .... of $13.5 million.
   e. We have 2,000 .... in twelve offices around the country.

   Check your answers in the key **9A.2**

9B Listening

You will hear the General Manager of Cerico SA giving a presentation on his company.

 Listen to cassette 9B.1 and complete the company profile.

Concentrate **only** on the information you need.

Play the cassette as many times as you want.

CERICO SA

Based in Seville, Spain

Main activity: exporting traditional Spanish ceramics
                                            (+ some manufacturing)

a.   main country markets: .... and ....

b.   value: £........................

c.   turnover: £........................

d.   pre-tax profits: £........................

e.   employees: ....

Check your answers in the key **9B.1**

9C Language check

1. Your company

Look at these sentences and write similar sentences about your company.

a. We're based in Seville.

b. Our main activity is exporting traditional hand-painted ceramics.

c. Our main markets are the UK and Germany.

d. We have 148 employees.

e. In the last financial year our turnover was £31 million.

f. Our pre-tax profits were £3.2 million.

g. The company has a value of £48.5 million.

2. Questions I

Finish re-writing these questions. Choose the correct word from the list to complete each one.

| turnover | value | employees | based | profits |

a. Where is the head office of your company?
Where is your company .... ?
b. How many people work for your company?
How many .... are there?
c. How much money did your company make last year?
What was your company's .... ?
What were your company's .... ?
d. How much is your company worth?
What's the .... of the company?

Now listen to cassette 9C.2.

Check your answers in the key **9C.2**

3. Questions 2

Finish writing these questions about Cerico so they match their answers.
a. What .... ?
Exporting traditional hand-painted ceramics.
b. Where .... ?
In Seville.
c. What .... ?
The UK and Germany.

Now listen to cassette 9C.3.

Check your answers in the key **9C.3**

9D Pronunciation

I. In these questions, the important stresses are underlined.

Listen to cassette 9D.1 and repeat to practise.
a. Where's the company based?
b. What's the main activity of the company?
c. What are the main markets?
d. How many employees are there?
e. What was last year's turnover?
f. What were the profits?
g. What's the value of the company?

2. Say these numbers.

a. 567 employees   c. 13 countries   e. $7.9m

b. 18 offices   d. $87.5m   f. $365m

Listen to cassette 9D.2 and repeat to practise.

Check your answers in the key **9D.2**

3. Listen to cassette 9D.3 and read silently.

> ACI is based in Sweden. Its main activity is exporting paper and its main markets are France and Italy. The company has 567 employees in 18 offices in 13 countries. The turnover last year was $87.5 million with profits of $7.9 million. The value of the company is $365 million.

4. Rewind the cassette to the beginning of 9D.3.

Listen and read aloud in time with the cassette.

Practise until you can keep the same rhythm and speed as the cassette.

9E Speaking

1. Look at this company profile.

Q and A Software

Location:	Oxford
Main activity:	designing and selling software
Main country markets:	Great Britain, the USA
Employees	87
Turnover:	£11,635,000
Pre-tax profits:	£1,651,000
Value of the company:	£21,000,000

Listen to cassette 9E.1.

You will hear seven questions about Q and A Software.

Answer the questions from the profile. After you answer, you will hear an example answer.

Follow the model.

QUESTION	Where's the company based?
YOU	In Oxford.
EXAMPLE	In Oxford.

2. Listen to cassette 9E.2.

This time **you** ask the questions and you will hear the Managing Director of Q and A Software answering them.

Follow the conversation plan and speak in the spaces.

Practise as many times as you want. The cassette will tell you when to start.

You

Managing Director

... based?

In Oxford.

... main activity ... ?

Designing and selling software.

... main country markets?

Great Britain and the USA.

... employees?

Eighty-seven.

... turnover?

Just over £11.5 million.

... pre-tax profits?

£1.65 million.

... value of the company?

£21 million.

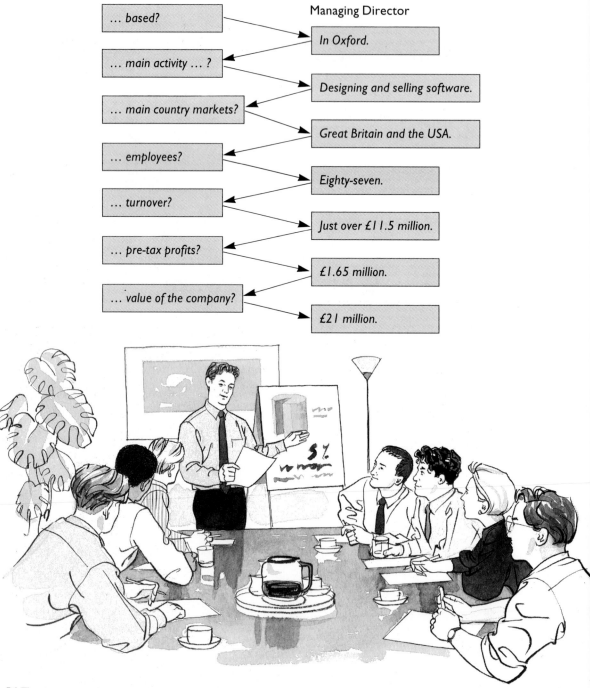

3. Use this chart to prepare some notes for a presentation on your company or another company you know well.

Notes	Information
... is located in ...	....
main activity/activities is/are ...	....
main market/markets is/are ...	....
has/have ... employees ...	....
in the last financial year turnover was ... with pre-tax profits of ...	....
... value of the company is ...	....

Record your presentation on a blank cassette. Then listen to it and give yourself a mark out of ten (ten = perfect). Think about your pronunciation, grammar, vocabulary and fluency.

Business trips

Language for

talking about past events and actions
asking questions about past events and actions

10A Preparation

Complete this table.

present	simple past
am/is/are	was/were
1.	did
go	2.
3.	had
say	4.
5.	told
take	6.
7.	got
can	8.
9.	gave
think	10.

Check your answers in the key **10A**

10B Listening

1. Janet Bryan has just come back from a sales trip. She is talking to a colleague, Hans Muller, about the trip.

Listen to cassette 10B.1 and answer the questions. Tick the correct boxes.

a. Which countries did she visit?

☐ France   ☐ Germany

☐ Italy   ☐ Austria

b. How long was the trip?

☐ one week   ☐ three weeks

☐ two weeks   ☐ four weeks

Check your answers in the key **10B.1**

2. Tim McBride is calling B and D White. He has some problems with an order.

What are the problems?

Listen to cassette 10B.2 and tick the correct boxes.

☐ It arrived late.   ☐ Part of the order was missing.

☐ It was damaged.   ☐ It was the wrong order.

Check your answers in the key **10B.2**

3. John Lucas meets Marie-Noëlle Cousin at the airport. Marie-Noëlle has just arrived from Prague.

Listen to cassette 10B.3 and answer the questions. Tick the correct boxes.

a. What time did she leave Prague?

☐ 8.00   ☐ 8.30

☐ 7.30   ☐ 7.00

b. Where did she have to change planes?

☐ Budapest   ☐ Berlin

☐ Rome   ☐ Vienna

Check your answers in the key **10B.3**

10C Language check

I. Irregular verbs

Look at Hans Muller's diary for last week.

MONDAY	TUESDAY	WEDNESDAY	THURSDAY	FRIDAY
9.30 Terry Marsden (CFG)	8.20 BA2131 to Manchester		Read Jerry Tyson's report	7.15 Train to Brighton
	10.00 Regional Marketing Meeting (two days)		Write notes for Selby and Bonham	9.30 Presentation to directors of Selby and Bonham presentation
Lunch: Françoise Dulac				
		20.25 BA3345 to London		Flowers for Alison!

Complete Hans Muller's description of his week with the simple past of the verbs in the box.

| buy   come   take   fly   give   go   have   meet   read   sleep   write |

On Monday I .... Terry Marsden of CFG in the morning and then
.... lunch with Françoise Dulac. I .... to Manchester on Tuesday
and .... to the regional marketing meeting. I .... at the Manchester
City Hilton and .... back the next day. On Thursday I .... Jerry
Tyson's report and .... the notes for my presentation. On Friday I
.... a train to Brighton and .... the presentation to the directors of
Selby and Bonham. On the way home I .... some flowers for Alison.

Now listen to cassette 10C.1.   *Check your answers in the key* **10C.1**

2. Questions

Look at Hans Muller's diary again. Put the words of these questions in the correct order.
Follow the example.

did/meet/Monday/morning/on/who/you ?	Who did you meet on Monday morning?

a. did/have/lunch/Monday/on/with/you/who ?
b. did/go/on/Tuesday/where/you ?
c. did/go/Manchester/to/why/you ?
d. back/did/fly/London/time/to/you/what ?
e. did/do/morning/on/Tuesday/what/you ?
f. Alison/buy/did/for/what/you ?

Now listen to cassette 10C.2.   *Check your answers in the key* **10C.2**

10D Pronunciation

1. In these questions, the important stresses are <u>underlined</u>.

Listen to cassette 10D.1 and repeat to practise.

   a. <u>Mon</u>day?

     on <u>Mon</u>day?

     <u>What</u> did you <u>do</u> on <u>Mon</u>day?

   b. <u>lunch</u>

     <u>lunch</u> <u>with</u>

     <u>Who</u> did you <u>have</u> <u>lunch</u> <u>with</u>?

   c. <u>flight</u>?

     a <u>good</u> <u>flight</u>?

     Did you <u>have</u> a <u>good</u> <u>flight</u>?

   d. <u>mee</u>ting?

     the <u>mee</u>ting?

     <u>How</u> was the <u>mee</u>ting?

   e. <u>week</u>?

     <u>last</u> <u>week</u>?

     <u>Where</u> were you <u>last</u> <u>week</u>?

2. Listen to cassette 10D.2 and <u>underline</u> the important stresses in each question.

   a. What time did you leave Prague? (four stresses)

   b. Did you have to change planes? (three stresses)

   c. Who did you fly with? (three stresses)

Check your answers in the key **10D.2**

3. Rewind the cassette to the beginning of 10D.2.

Listen and read aloud in time with the cassette.

Practise until you can keep the same rhythm and speed as the cassette.

10E Speaking

1. Listen to cassette 10E.1.

A sales manager is meeting a client at the airport.

2. Listen to cassette 10E.2.

This time you will hear only the client. **You** are the sales manager.

Follow the conversation plan and speak in the spaces.

Practise as many times as you want.

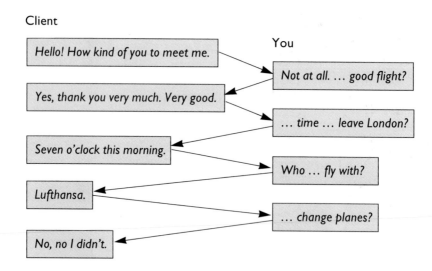

3. You have just been away on a business trip. You were away for two weeks. You visited New York, Chicago and San Francisco. A colleague is going to ask you three questions about your trip.

Listen to cassette 10E.3 and answer his questions. After your conversation, you will hear an example conversation.

4. You received an order of 200 bearings for your factory this morning but the bearings are the wrong type. You wanted 3 mm not 4 mm bearings. You phone your supplier, B and D White.

Listen to cassette 10E.4. Follow the conversation plan and speak in the spaces.

After your conversation, you will hear an example conversation.

B and D White

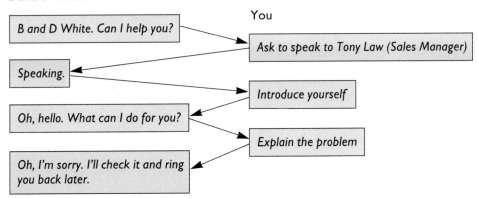

You

| B and D White. Can I help you? |
| Ask to speak to Tony Law (Sales Manager) |
| Speaking. |
| Introduce yourself |
| Oh, hello. What can I do for you? |
| Explain the problem |
| Oh, I'm sorry. I'll check it and ring you back later. |

5. Listen to cassette 10E.5.

You will hear five questions about what you did last week. Answer the questions.

Speak in the spaces and use real information about your appointments and activities.

UNIT 11

Instructions

Language for
giving and understanding instructions

11A Preparation

Listen to cassette 11A and read silently. What is the machine in these instructions?

> Put your card in the machine and type your personal identification number (PIN). Choose WITHDRAW CASH from the menu and type the amount you want. Wait a few seconds for the operation to finish. Take your card, your money and the advice slip.

Check your answers in the key **11A**

11B Listening

1. Listen to cassette 11B.1.

You will hear three sets of instructions. Which picture goes with which instructions?

a.

b.

c.

d.

Check your answers in the key **11B.1**

2. Dominic Lasalle works for Abbot, Lyon and Chang, a consultancy company. He has just completed his first sales call.

Look at his client's business card and complete as much of the report card as possible.

John Lord
Distribution Manager

Hart Components

19 Barracks Hill, London SW19
Tel: (81) 218 9098
Fax: (81) 218 7632

Abbot, Lyon and Chang
SALES CALL REPORT CARD

Name		Dates of visits	
		Contact name	
Address		Position	
		Decision maker	yes / no
		If no	Name of decision maker
			Position of decision maker
Tel:			
Fax:		Initiated by	Client / ALC

Now listen to cassette 11B.2.

Dominic's boss, Juliet Leham, is helping him with the rest of the report card.

Complete the missing information.

Check your answers in the key **11B.2**

11C Language check

1. Imperatives

In English, the imperative has the same form as the infinitive without **to**.

> Press the button on the front.
> Wait a few seconds.

We sometimes use **you** with the imperative.

> Then you turn on the monitor.

We make the negative like this.

> Don't press that button.

We use the imperative for instructions.

Note: In English, we do not usually use the imperative when we ask for things. It is not very polite to say: *Give me a pen*. It is much better to say: *Can you give me a pen?*

Complete these instructions for turning on a video with the imperative of the verbs in the box.

> press   set   put   turn on   move

.... in the cassette at the front of the VCR. .... the TV and .... the channel to ZERO. .... the switch on the top of the remote control to VCR. .... PLAY, and it starts.

Check your answers in the key **11C.1**

2. Simple instructions

Look at the picture and put the instructions for starting a car into a logical order.

☐ a. press the clutch
☐ b. and release the handbrake
☐ c. at the same time, release the clutch
☐ d. check you're in neutral
☐ e. put the car in first
☐ f. press the accelerator slowly
☐ g. turn the key in the ignition and press the accelerator to start the engine

Now listen to cassette 11C.2.

Check your answers in the key **11C.2**

3. Complex instructions

when/where + present simple + imperative

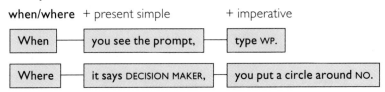

| When | — | you see the prompt, | — | type WP. |

| Where | — | it says DECISION MAKER, | — | you put a circle around NO. |

Look at this plan and write instructions for using a cash machine.
Follow the example.

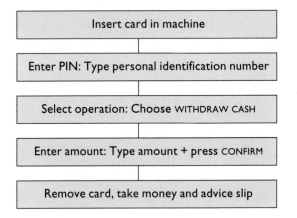

| Insert card in machine |

| Enter PIN: Type personal identification number |

| Select operation: Choose WITHDRAW CASH |

| Enter amount: Type amount + press CONFIRM |

| Remove card, take money and advice slip |

Enter PIN: When you see ENTER PIN, type your personal identification number.

a. Select operation:

b. Enter amount:

 Now listen to cassette 11C.3.

 Check your answers in the key **11C.3**

4. A fax

Look at this fax and write instructions for completing the first part.

Follow the example.

Hart Components   FAX MESSAGE

To: Abbot, Lyon and Change   *Date:*   27th August
Attention: Dominic Lasalle   *Pages:*   5 (including this)
From: John Lord

If you do not receive all the pages, please contact us immediately on (81) 218 9098.

Dear Dominic,

I'm sending you some information about our computer systems.

Regards,

John Lord

To: Where it says TO, put the name of the company you are sending the fax to.

a. Attention: c. Date:
b. From: d. Pages:

Now listen to cassette 11C.4.

Check your answers in the key   **11C.4**

11D Pronunciation

1. In these sentences, the important stresses are <u>underlined</u>.

Listen to cassette 11D.1 and repeat to practise.
    a. <u>Put</u> the cass<u>ette</u> <u>in</u>.   e. <u>Check</u> you're in <u>neu</u>tral.
    b. <u>Turn</u> <u>on</u> the <u>tele</u>vision.   f. <u>Move</u> the <u>gear</u> <u>lever</u>.
    c. <u>Set</u> the <u>channel</u> to **zero**.   g. Re<u>lease</u> the <u>clutch</u>.
    d. <u>Press</u> the <u>button</u> on the <u>front</u>.

2. Listen to cassette 11D.2 and <u>underline</u> the most important stresses in each sentence.
    a. When you see ENTER PIN (four stresses), type your personal identification number (four stresses).
    b. When you see SELECT OPERATION (four stresses), choose WITHDRAW CASH (three stresses).
    c. When you see ENTER AMOUNT (four stresses), type the amount of money you want and press CONFIRM (six stresses).

Check your answers in the key   **11D.2**

3. Rewind the cassette to the beginning of 11D.2.

Listen and read aloud in time with the cassette.

Practise until you can keep the same rhythm and speed as the cassette.

11E Speaking

Use the pictures and vocabulary notes to give instructions for
1. Writing an English cheque
2. Sending a fax
3. Doing a three-point turn

1. How to write an English cheque

> **VOCABULARY**
> amount, put, sign, words, figures, top, bottom, second, right, line

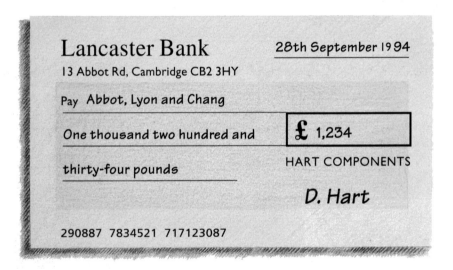

2. How to send a fax from the machine in your office

> **VOCABULARY**
> dial, wait, engage, light, come on, document

3. How to do a three-point turn

VOCABULARY
steering wheel, turn, brake, gear, reverse, first, mirror, clutch

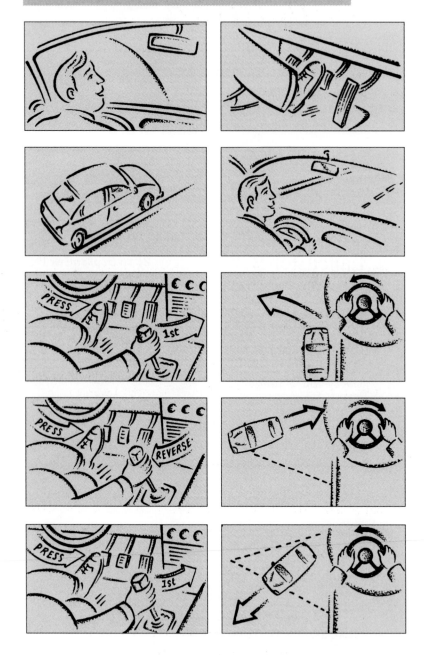

Now listen to cassette 11E.1.

You will hear example instructions.

Play them as many times as you want and repeat to practise.

Competition

Language for

talking about competitors
making comparisons

12A Preparation

Complete this text. Choose the correct word/s from each box to make true sentences about your company.

> One of our main competitors is .... Their share of the market is
>
> | larger / smaller | than ours | and / but | their profits are | higher / about the same / lower | Their | products / services | are |
>
> | more / less | expensive than ours | but / and | their quality is | better / about the same / worse |

12B Listening

1. You will hear Lauren Kier, Chief Executive Officer (CEO) of ACE, a computer hardware company, talking to a consultant about StarLinea, one of ACE's main competitors.

   Listen to cassette 12B.1 and answer the questions. Tick the correct boxes.

   Concentrate **only** on the information you need to answer the questions.

   Play the conversation as many times as you want.

	ACE	StarLinea
a. Which company's products are more expensive?	☐	☐
b. Which company's products are better quality?	☐	☐
c. Which company has a larger share of the market?	☐	☐

   Check your answers in the key **12B.1**

2. Now you will hear Lauren Kier talking to the consultant about this chart.

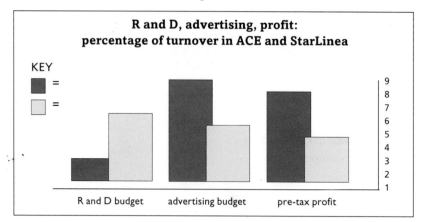

Listen to cassette 12B.2 and complete the key. Which company do the blue bars represent and which company do the grey bars represent?

Check your answers in the key **12B.2**

12C Language check

1. Comparisons

The most usual way to make comparisons in English is to use comparative adjectives.

With short adjectives, you form the comparative by adding **-(e)r** to the end: large – larger; small – smaller.

> Graphic's market share is **larger**.
> Q.Print's market share is **smaller**.

With longer adjectives, you form the comparative by putting *more* or **less** before the adjective: profitable – more profitable, less profitable.

> Graphic is **more profitable**.
> Q.Print is **less profitable**.

Good and **bad** have irregular forms: good – better, bad – worse.

> The offer from Graphic is **better**.
> The offer from Q.Print is **worse**.

To connect the two things or ideas we are comparing, we use **than** (pronounced /ðen/).

> Graphic's market share is **larger than** Q.Print's.
> Q.Print's market share is **smaller than** Graphic's.
> Graphic is **more profitable than** Q.Print.
> Q.Print is **less profitable than** Graphic.
> The offer from Graphic is **better than** the offer from Q.Print.
> The offer from Q.Print is **worse than** the offer from Graphic.

Complete this chart. Which adjectives form the comparative with **-(e)r** and which with **more/less**?

	a. -(e)r (than)	b. more/less (than)
cheap		
economical		
expensive		
high		
large		
low		
profitable		
quick		

Now correct the mistakes in these sentences.
c. Graphic is more cheap than Q.Print.
d. Q.Print is less profitabler than Graphic.
e. Graphic's turnover is larger that Q.Print's.
f. The quality of Graphic's work is more good.

Check your answers in the key **12C.1**

2. Look at the chart.

a.	Tokyo	expensive	The Eiffel Tower
b.	A Porsche	big	spending
c.	The Hilton	fast	a Volvo
d.	The Empire State Building	difficult	Marseilles
e.	Saving	tall	The Holiday Inn

Use the ideas in the chart to make complete sentences. Use each idea once.

Follow the example.

Tokyo is bigger than Marseilles.

Now listen to cassette 12C.2

Check your answers in the key **12C.2**

3. Comparing competitors

Look at this table.

	ACE	StarLinea
Market share	22%	19%
Turnover	$450m	$370m
Pre-tax profit	$12.6m (3%)	$26m (7%)
R and D budget	$22.5m (5%)	$3.7m (1%)
Advertising budget	$18m (4%)	$29.6m (8%)
Product quality	*****	****
Pricing policy	high	medium

Use these notes and the information in the table to make sentences comparing the two companies.

Follow the example.

ACE's market share / large / StarLinea's   ACE's market share is larger than StarLinea's.

---

a. ACE's turnover / high / StarLinea's
b. ACE / profitable / StarLinea
c. ACE's R and D budget / high / StarLinea's
d. ACE's advertising budget / low / StarLinea's
e. ACE's products / good quality / StarLinea's
f. ACE's products / expensive / StarLinea's

 Now listen to cassette 12C.2.

Check your answers in the key **12C.2**

12D Pronunciation

1. In these words, the important stress is <u>underlined</u>.

Listen to cassette 12D.1 and repeat to practise.
a. <u>tur</u>nover
b. <u>ad</u>vertising
c. <u>qua</u>lity
d. <u>bud</u>get
e. <u>mar</u>ket
f. <u>pro</u>fitable
g. ex<u>pen</u>sive
h. <u>lar</u>ger
i. <u>smal</u>ler
j. <u>high</u>er
k. <u>low</u>er

2. Listen to cassette 12D.2 and <u>underline</u> the stresses in each sentence.

    a. ACE's market share is larger than StarLinea's. (five stresses)

    b. ACE's turnover is higher than StarLinea's. (four stresses)

    c. ACE is less profitable than StarLinea. (four stresses)

    d. ACE's R and D budget is higher than StarLinea's. (six stresses)

    e. ACE's advertising budget is lower than StarLinea's. (five stresses)

    f. ACE's products are better quality than StarLinea's. (five stresses)

    g. ACE's products are more expensive than StarLinea's. (five stresses)

3. Rewind the cassette to the beginning of 12D.2.

Listen and speak in time with the cassette.

Practise until you can keep the same rhythm and speed as the cassette.

12E Speaking

1. Listen to cassette 12E.1.

A journalist from the business press is interviewing ACE's CEO, Lauren Kier.

2. Listen to cassette 12E.2.

This time you will hear only the journalist. **You** are ACE's CEO.

Follow the conversation plan and speak in the spaces.

Practise as many times as you want.

Journalist

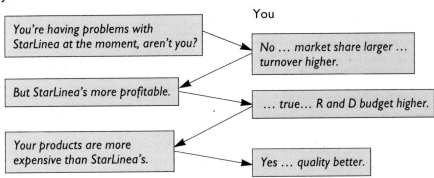

Journalist

You're having problems with StarLinea at the moment, aren't you?

But StarLinea's more profitable.

Your products are more expensive than StarLinea's.

You

No ... market share larger ... turnover higher.

... true... R and D budget higher.

Yes ... quality better.

3. The same journalist is going to ask **you** some questions about **your** company and its main competitor.

Listen to cassette 12E.3 and answer the questions.

4. Choose a company you know well and one of its main competitors.

Give a short presentation comparing the two companies. Talk about quality, price, market share and turnover.

Record yourself on a blank cassette. Then listen and give yourself a mark out of ten (ten perfect). Think about your pronunciation, grammar, vocabulary and fluency.

Answer key

UNIT I

Arriving for an appointment

1B Listening

IB.I

Times	Visitors	Managers
10.30	Eileen Wade	Jenny Saunders
12.00	John Morgan	Mark Roberts
15.00	Irene Tate	Jeff Hartley
16.30	Andrew Moncourt	Simone Canning

IB.2

a. Andrew Moncourt; Eileen Wade
b. John Morgan – traffic was terrible; Irene Tate – plane delayed
c. Andrew Moncourt – a few minutes; Irene Tate – about twenty minutes

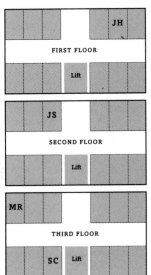

IB

Conversation I

RECEPTIONIST: Good morning. Can I help you?

EILEEN WADE: Good morning. I've got an appointment with Jenny Saunders.

RECEPTIONIST: What time is she expecting you?

EILEEN WADE: Ten-thirty.

RECEPTIONIST: Could I have your name, please?

EILEEN WADE: Eileen Wade.

RECEPTIONIST: Just a moment. *(picks up phone)* Jenny? Ms Wade's here to see you. Yes, OK. *(to Eileen Wade)* She's free to see you now. Do you know where her office is?

EILEEN WADE: No, I don't.

RECEPTIONIST: It's on the second floor. Come out of the lift, turn left and it's the first door on your right.

EILEEN WADE: Thank you very much.

RECEPTIONIST: Not at all.

Conversation 2

RECEPTIONIST: Good morning. Can I help you?

JOHN MORGAN: Good morning. I've got an appointment with Mark Roberts at twelve o'clock. I'm afraid I'm a little late: the traffic was terrible.

RECEPTIONIST: Could I have your name?

JOHN MORGAN: Morgan, John Morgan.

RECEPTIONIST: Just a moment. *(picks up phone)* Mark? Mr Morgan's here. *(to John Morgan)* He'll see you now, Mr Morgan. Do you know where his office is?

JOHN MORGAN: No, I don't.

RECEPTIONIST: It's on the third floor. Come out of the lift, turn left and it's the third door on your right.

JOHN MORGAN: Thank you.

RECEPTIONIST: Not at all.

Conversation 3

RECEPTIONIST: Good afternoon. Can I help you?

IRENE TATE: Good afternoon. I've got an appointment with Jeff Hartley at three o'clock. I'm terribly sorry, I'm afraid I'm very late. My flight was delayed.

RECEPTIONIST: I'm afraid he's in a meeting now. Could I have your name?

IRENE TATE: Irene Tate. How long will he be?

RECEPTIONIST: About twenty minutes. Can you wait?

IRENE TATE: Certainly, of course.

(twenty minutes later)

RECEPTIONIST: Ms Tate?

IRENE TATE: Yes?

RECEPTIONIST: Mr Hartley's free now. Do you know where his office is?

IRENE TATE: No.

RECEPTIONIST: It's on the first floor. Come out of the lift, turn right and it's the second door on your left.

IRENE TATE: Thank you.

RECEPTIONIST: Not at all.

Conversation 4

RECEPTIONIST: Good afternoon. Can I help you?

ANDREW MONCOURT: Good afternoon. I've got an appointment with Simone Canning. My name's Andrew Moncourt.

RECEPTIONIST: What time is she expecting you, Mr Moncourt?

ANDREW MONCOURT: Half past four.

RECEPTIONIST: Just a moment: I'll see if she's free.

ANDREW MONCOURT: Thank you.

RECEPTIONIST: *(picks up phone)* Simone? Jenny, is Simone there? Oh. Well, when she's finished, can you tell her Mr Moncourt's waiting in reception? Thank you. *(to Andrew Moncourt)* I'm afraid she's on the phone at the moment. Can you wait a few minutes?

ANDREW MONCOURT: Certainly.

(a few minutes later)

RECEPTIONIST: *(answers phone)* Hello? Hello, Simone. Right you are. *(to Andrew Moncourt)* Mr Moncourt?

ANDREW MONCOURT: Yes?

RECEPTIONIST: Ms Canning's free now. Do you know where her office is?

ANDREW MONCOURT: No.

RECEPTIONIST: It's on the third floor. Come out of the lift, turn left and it's the first door on your left.

ANDREW MONCOURT: Thank you.

RECEPTIONIST: Not at all.

1C Language check

1C 📼

The missing words are in **bold**.

RECEPTIONIST: Good morning. Can I **help** you?

VISITOR: Yes. I've got an **appointment** with Annette Rawstern.

RECEPTIONIST: What time is she **expecting** you?

VISITOR: Ten o'clock.

RECEPTIONIST: Could I have your **name**, please?

VISITOR: John Wilson.

RECEPTIONIST: Take a seat. I'll see if she's **free**.

VISITOR: Thank you.

RECEPTIONIST: I'm **afraid** she's on the phone at the moment. Could you **wait** a few minutes?

VISITOR: Certainly.

(a few minutes later)

RECEPTIONIST: You can go up now. Do you know where her **office** is?

VISITOR: Er, no.

RECEPTIONIST: It's on the third **floor**. Come out of the **lift**, turn right and it's the second on the left.

VISITOR: Thank you.

RECEPTIONIST: Not at all.

1D Pronunciation

1D.2 📼

a. It's the <u>first</u> <u>door</u> on the <u>right</u>.
b. It's the <u>second</u> <u>door</u> on the <u>left</u>.
c. It's the <u>third</u> <u>door</u> on the <u>left</u>.
d. It's the <u>third</u> <u>door</u> on the <u>right</u>.

1D.3 📼

a. Could I <u>have</u> your <u>name</u>, <u>please</u>?
b. I'll <u>see</u> if he's <u>free</u>.
c. Can you <u>tell</u> me <u>where</u> his <u>office</u> is?
d. I'm a<u>fraid</u> she's on the <u>phone</u> at the <u>moment</u>.

1E Speaking

1E.1 📼

QUESTION 2: Can you tell me where Jean Wright's office is?

YOU: ....

EXAMPLE: *Come out of the lift, turn left and it's the second door on the left.*

QUESTION 3: Can you tell me where Alice Rowan's office is?

YOU: ....

EXAMPLE: *Come out of the lift, turn left and it's the second door on the right.*

QUESTION 4: Can you tell me where Peter Knight's office is?

YOU: ....

EXAMPLE: *Come out of the lift, turn left and it's the third door on the right.*

QUESTION 5: Can you tell me where Dominic Lowe's office is?

YOU: ....

EXAMPLE: *Come out of the lift, turn right and it's the first door on the left.*

QUESTION 6: Can you tell me where Terry Bevan's office is?

YOU: ....

EXAMPLE: *Come out of the lift, turn right and it's the third door on the right.*

UNIT 2
First conversations

2A Preparation

2A

l. c; 2. e; 3. a; 4. b; 5. f; 6. d

2B Listening

2B.1 📼

The expressions are in **bold**.

CAROL BERKELEY: Jean-Claude, let me introduce you to George. George, this is Jean-Claude Duval. Jean-Claude works with me in New York.

GEORGE ROTHERFORD: **How do you do?**

JEAN-CLAUDE DUVAL: **Pleased to meet you**. Are you the …

Note: *How do you do?* is not really a question. It means the same as *Pleased to meet you*. We only use it the first time we meet a person.

2B.2

a. Australian
b. engineer
c. Panasonic
d. Canada

2B.2 📼

GEORGE ROTHERFORD: I'm sorry, I didn't catch your name. You're … ?

JEAN-CLAUDE DUVAL: Jean-Claude.

GEORGE ROTHERFORD: I'm George. Where are you from? France?

JEAN-CLAUDE DUVAL: Yes, that's right. And you, are you English?

GEORGE ROTHERFORD: No, I'm Australian, but I left Australia ten years ago.

JEAN-CLAUDE DUVAL: So, where do you live now?

GEORGE ROTHERFORD: Well, in Canada, actually.

JEAN-CLAUDE DUVAL: That must be very interesting. What do you do there?

GEORGE ROTHERFORD: Oh, I'm an engineer.

JEAN-CLAUDE DUVAL: Who do you work for?

GEORGE ROTHERFORD: Panasonic. I've been there for about …

2B.3

a. True   b. True   c. False

2B.3 📼

JEAN-CLAUDE DUVAL: So, where do you know Carol from?

GEORGE ROTHERFORD: Oh, we worked together at Sony in Australia: marvellous person.

JEAN-CLAUDE DUVAL: Yes, she is.

GEORGE ROTHERFORD: Do you like New York?

JEAN-CLAUDE DUVAL: Yes, I do, but I haven't been there very long. Have you ever been to the USA?

GEORGE ROTHERFORD: No, I haven't. Let me get you a drink. What would you like?

JEAN-CLAUDE DUVAL: Oh, I'll have a Perrier, please. Thank you very much.

2C Language check

2C.1

a. vii; b. v; c. iv; d. iii; e. i; f. vi; g.ii

2C.1 📼

Where are you from? Holland, originally.

Where do you live? Milan, at the moment.

What do you do? I'm an engineer.

Do you like Milan? Yes, I do.

Who do you work for? Hewlett-Packard.

Where do you know Anne from? We worked together at Microsoft.

Have you ever been to Italy? Yes, I have.

2C.3 📼

The missing words are in **bold**.

A: Where do you live?

B: In Montreal. **Have you ever been to** Canada?

A: Yes, **I have**. I **went to** Quebec on business last year. **Have you ever been to** Quebec?

B: No, **I haven't**.

2C.5 📼

a. Where do you know Peter from?
b. Where do you know Abdul from?
c. Where do you know Hans from?

2C.6

These are some possibilities.

We worked together at (Microsoft). We met at a party. We met at university. She's/He's a friend of my wife/husband. We worked on a project together. We're both in the same sports club. We play (tennis) together. We met when we were doing military service. Our families were friends. We went to school together. We met on holiday. We're neighbours.

2D Pronunciation

2D.2 📼

a. Do you <u>like</u> <u>Paris</u>?
b. Do you <u>like</u> <u>London</u>?
c. Do you <u>like</u> <u>Tokyo</u>?

2D.3 📼

a. Have you <u>ever</u> <u>been</u> to <u>Great</u> <u>Britain</u>?
b. Have you <u>ever</u> <u>been</u> to the <u>USA</u>?
c. Have you <u>ever</u> <u>been</u> to Aust<u>ra</u>lia?

2D.4 📼

a. <u>Where</u> are you <u>from</u>?
b. <u>Where</u> do you <u>live</u>?
c. <u>What</u> do you <u>do</u>?
d. <u>Who</u> do you <u>work</u> <u>for</u>?
e. <u>Where</u> do you <u>know</u> <u>Anne</u> <u>from</u>?

UNIT 3

Names and numbers

3B Listening

3B.1

a. Xavier Bereciartua
b. Dominique Gureghian
c. Sandra Fayette
d. Nina Trufanow

3B.1 📼

Conversation 1

CLERK: Could you give me your name, please?
XAVIER: Xavier Bereciartua.
CLERK: Could you spell that?
XAVIER: Xavier X–A–V I–E–R.
CLERK: OK.
XAVIER: Bereciartua B–E–R …
CLERK: Did you say **B** or **V**?
XAVIER: B, B for … Barcelona.
CLERK: OK.
XAVIER: B–E–R E–C …
CLERK: E–C. Right.
XAVIER: I–A–R …
CLERK: Aha.
XAVIER: T–U–A.
CLERK: T–U–A. Thank you.

Conversation 2

CLERK: Could you give me your name, please?
DOMINIQUE: Dominique Gureghian.
CLERK: Could you spell that?
DOMINIQUE: Dominique D–O–M I–N …
CLERK: Did you say **N** or **M**?
DOMINIQUE: N for Naples. D–O–M I–N …
CLERK: Right.
DOMINIQUE: I–Q–U–E.
CLERK: OK.
DOMINIQUE: Gureghian G–U–R E–G H–I–A–N.
CLERK: G–U–R E–G H–I–A–N.
DOMINIQUE: That's right.

Conversation 3

CLERK: Could you give me your name, please?
SANDRA: Sandra Fayette.
CLERK: Sandra … ?
SANDRA: Fayette.
CLERK: Could you spell that?
SANDRA: Sandra S–A–N D–R–A.
CLERK: Right.
SANDRA: Fayette F-A-Y …
CLERK: Yes.
SANDRA: E–T–T–E.
CLERK: E–T–T–E.
SANDRA: That's right.

Conversation 4

CLERK: Could you give me your name, please?
NINA: Nina Trufanow.
CLERK: Could you spell that?
NINA: Nina N–I–N–A.
CLERK: Fine. And your surname?
NINA: Trufanow. T–R–U F–A–N O–W.
CLERK: T–R–U F–A–N O–W.
NINA: That's right.

3B.2

213 4051; 788 5492; 601 2133

3B.2 📼

Conversation 1

A: Could I have your phone number?
B: It's two one three, four oh five one.
A: Two one three … ?
B: Four oh five one.
A: Thank you.

Conversation 2

A: Could I have your phone number?
C: It's seven double eight, five four nine two.
A: Seven double eight, five four nine two.
C: That's right.

Conversation 3

A: Could I have your phone number?
D: It's six oh one …
A: Sorry, did you say **six**?
D: That's right – six oh one.
A: Carry on.
D: Two one double three.
A: Six oh one, two one double three.
D: That's right.

3B.3

a.

ADDRESS	TEL
John Walsh	71 344 6612.
BCI Books,	**FAX**
125 Chorister Road,	71 344 0188.
London	
W1A 9HJ	

b.

ADDRESS	TEL
Le Trumalu,	617 980 7702
15 Schroeder Park,	**FAX**
Boston,	
Massachusetts	
12116.	

3B.3 📼

Conversation 1

RECEPTIONIST: Good morning. Infomat, can I help you?

JOHN WALSH: Good morning. I saw your advertisement in the paper. I was wondering if you could send me a catalogue.
RECEPTIONIST: Certainly. Could you give me your name and address, please?
JOHN WALSH: It's John Walsh of BCI Books.
RECEPTIONIST: I'm sorry, what did you say was the name of the company?
JOHN WALSH: BCI Books.
RECEPTIONIST: And the address?
JOHN WALSH: One two five Chorister Road.
RECEPTIONIST: How do you spell Chorister?
JOHN WALSH: C–H–O–R I–S T–E–R.
RECEPTIONIST: C–H–O–R I–S T–E–R.
JOHN WALSH: Aha.
RECEPTIONIST: And that was one two five?
JOHN WALSH: That's right. And it's London W–one–A nine–H–J.
RECEPTIONIST: W–one–A nine–H–J. Could you give me your telephone number, please?
JOHN WALSH: Seven one, three double four, double six one two.
RECEPTIONIST: Do you have a fax number?
JOHN WALSH: Yes … seven one, three double four, oh one double eight.
RECEPTIONIST: Thank you very much. We'll put it in the post today.
JOHN WALSH: Thank you. Goodbye.
RECEPTIONIST: Goodbye.

Conversation 2

FRAN: Hello.
JEANETTE: Hi, Fran. This is Jeanette. How are you?
FRAN: Fine. What can I do for you?
JEANETTE: Fran, I've got this trip to Boston next week to see Larry Mezure.
FRAN: Yes.
JEANETTE: I wanted to take him out for lunch. Do you know any good restaurants in Boston?
FRAN: Well, do you know Le Trumalu?
JEANETTE: No, what's it like?
FRAN: It's nice. It's a French restaurant.
JEANETTE: Let me get a pencil. What was the name again?
FRAN: Le Trumalu.
JEANETTE: How do you spell that?
FRAN: T–R–U M–A L–U.
JEANETTE: Aha. What's the address?
FRAN: Fifteen Schroeder Park, Boston one two one one six.
JEANETTE: Sorry?
FRAN: S–C–H–R O–E–D E–R Park. Schroeder Park.
JEANETTE: S–C–H–R O–E–D E–R.

FRAN: That's right.

JEANETTE: And it was number fifteen?

FRAN: Yes. Do you want the phone number?

JEANETTE: Please.

FRAN: It's six one seven for Boston, nine eight zero, seven seven zero two.

JEANETTE: Did you say **nine** eight zero or **five** eight zero?

FRAN: Nine eight zero.

JEANETTE: OK. Thanks very much.

FRAN: Not at all. Have a nice trip. Hope you enjoy the restaurant.

JEANETTE: Thanks. Bye.

FRAN: Bye.

3C Language check

3C.I 📼

a. Could you give me your name?

b. Could you spell that?

c. Could you speak a little more slowly?

d. Could you give me your address?

e. Could you give me your phone number?

f. I'm sorry, what did you say?

g. What's your fax number?

h. I'm sorry, did you say **six** or **seven**?

i. I'm sorry, could you speak up a little?

3C.2 📼

RECEPTIONIST: Could you give me your name?

CALLER: George Smith.

RECEPTIONIST: I'm sorry, what did you say?

CALLER: George Smith.

RECEPTIONIST: Could you spell that?

CALLER: S–M–I–T–H.

RECEPTIONIST: Could you give me your phone number?

CALLER: Four three nine eight, four five three two.

RECEPTIONIST: Could you speak a little more slowly?

CALLER: Four three nine eight, four five three two.

RECEPTIONIST: Could you give me your address?

CALLER: Six, rue St Lazare, seven five oh double one Paris.

RECEPTIONIST: I'm sorry, did you say six or seven?

CALLER: Six.

RECEPTIONIST: I'm sorry, could you speak up a little?

CALLER: Six.

RECEPTIONIST: What's your fax number?

CALLER: Four three nine eight, two one double eight.

3D Pronunciation

3D.2 📼

a. Could you <u>give</u> me your <u>address</u>?

b. Could you <u>give</u> me your <u>phone</u> number?

c. Could you <u>give</u> me your <u>fax</u> number?

3D.3 📼

a. Did you say **four** or **five**?

b. Did you say **five** or **nine**?

c. Did you say **nine** or **one**?

3D.5 📼

a. Could you <u>speak</u> more <u>slowly</u>?

b. Could you <u>speak</u> <u>up</u> a <u>little</u>?

c. Could you <u>spell</u> <u>that</u>?

3D.8 📼

a. six seven one, nine three five two

b. four oh four, eight seven double six

c. three nine zero, double two double nine

d. two three oh, five double one three

e. seven one five, treble six one

f. two three five, five nine double eight

3E Speaking

3E.I 📼

QUESTION 2: What's the fax number for Q and A Software?

YOU: ....

EXAMPLE: *seven six oh, eight seven double two*

QUESTION 3: What's the phone number of Santini Distribution?

YOU: ....

EXAMPLE: *nine eight one, oh two three two*

QUESTION 4: And their fax number?

YOU: ....

EXAMPLE: *nine eight one, double four double six*

QUESTION 5: What's the phone number for Royal Crest Insurance?

YOU: ....

EXAMPLE: *six double eight, eight zero double nine*

QUESTION 6: And their fax number?

YOU: ....

EXAMPLE: *six double eight, two three seven one*

QUESTION 7: What's the phone number of Cross Office Cleaning?

YOU: ....

EXAMPLE: *four six five, nine one three one*

QUESTION 8: And their fax number?

YOU: ....

EXAMPLE: *four six five, double oh one nine*

3E.2 📼

QUESTION 2: How do you spell professional?

YOU: ....

EXAMPLE: *P–R–O F–E–double S I–O–N–A–L*

QUESTION 3: How do you spell parallel?

YOU: ....

EXAMPLE: *P–A–R A–double L E–L*

QUESTION 4: How do you spell rhythm?

YOU: ....

EXAMPLE: *R–H–Y–T–H–M*

QUESTION 5: How do you spell personnel?

YOU: ....

EXAMPLE: *P–E–R S–O–double N–E–L*

UNIT 4

Telephone messages

4A Preparation

4A

1. c; 2. b; 3. d; 4. a

4B Listening

4B.1

Time: 11.30 not 11.00; tel: 43 82 54 not 43 82 45.

4B.1 📼

RECEPTIONIST: Crossways. Good afternoon. Can I help you?

JOHN COLLIS: Good afternoon. Could I speak to Lindy Cohen, please?

RECEPTIONIST: I'm afraid she's out at the moment. Can I take a message?

JOHN COLLIS: Yes, this is John Collis. I'm calling from Germany. I'm ringing about Ms Cohen's visit to Germany next week.

RECEPTIONIST: Yes.

JOHN COLLIS: Can you ask her if we can change the time of the marketing meeting on the first day? It was at ten o'clock, but that's a bit difficult for some of the participants.

RECEPTIONIST: What time would you prefer?

JOHN COLLIS: Well, eleven-thirty would be the best

time for us. Can you ask her to call me this afternoon?

RECEPTIONIST: Certainly. Could you give me your name?

JOHN COLLIS: Collis. C–O–double L–I–S.

RECEPTIONIST: And your number?

JOHN COLLIS: Four three, eight two, five four.

RECEPTIONIST: Four three, eight two, five four. She should be back soon. What time would you like her to call?

JOHN COLLIS: Any time in the afternoon until about six.

RECEPTIONIST: Very well. I'll see that she gets the message.

JOHN COLLIS: Thank you. Goodbye.

RECEPTIONIST: Goodbye.

4B.2

The missing words are in **bold**.

Greta rang. She'd like to meet for **dinner** next week on **Thursday**. Call her any evening after **6.30 p.m.** Tel: **45 63 22**.

4B.2 📼

LINDY COHEN: This is Lindy Cohen's number. I'm not at home at the moment, but if you'd like to leave your name and your telephone number, I'll call you back as soon as I can. *(beep)*

GRETA HASS: Lindy, this is Greta. As you're going to be in Munich next week, I was wondering if you'd like to meet for dinner some time. I'll be free on Thursday, if that's OK with you. Call me at home in the evening: I usually get back from the office at about six-thirty. Oh yes, I almost forgot. I've got a new phone number. It's Munich four five, six three, double two. I'll say it again: four five, six three, double two. Bye.

4B.3

Message for: Lindy Cohen
From: Ben Mitchell, OCA
Please call him as soon as possible about the new catalogue. Tel: 37 65 08.

4B.3 📼

CROSSWAYS: You have telephoned Crossways Shipping on seven one, three oh two, six seven five four. I'm afraid we can't take your call right now, but if you'd like to leave your name, your telephone number and a brief message, we'll call you back. Please speak after the tone. Thank you. *(beep)*

BEN MITCHELL: This is Ben Mitchell, M–I–T C–H–E–double L, of OCA. I'd like to speak to Lindy Cohen. I'm ringing about the new catalogue. Could she call me as soon as possible? My number's three seven, six five, oh eight. Thanks.

4C Language check

4C.1 📼

RECEPTIONIST: Hawker Robins. Good morning. Can I help you?

CALLER: Could I speak to Phil Allison, please?

RECEPTIONIST: One moment... I'm afraid he's in a meeting. Can I take a message?

CALLER: Yes. Could you ask him to call me before four o'clock? I'm ringing about the AJK proposal.

RECEPTIONIST: Certainly. Could I have your name, please?

CALLER: John Leblique.

RECEPTIONIST: How do you spell that?

CALLER: L–E–B L–I Q–U–E.

RECEPTIONIST: And your number?

CALLER: Four five three, two one two one.

RECEPTIONIST: I'll see that he gets your message.

CALLER: Thank you very much. Goodbye.

RECEPTIONIST: Goodbye.

4C.2 📼

The missing words are in **bold**.

This is Mark Levy of AGC. **I'd like to speak to** John Benson. **I'm ringing about** the marketing meeting. **Could he call me** as soon as possible? **My number's** seven five six, eight three four three. Thanks.

4C.3 📼

a. Could you ask her to call me after three o'clock?
b. Could you ask him to call me before five o'clock?
c. Could you ask him to send me a fax tomorrow morning?
d. Could you ask her to get in touch as soon as possible?

4D Pronunciation

4D.2 📼

a. I'm ringing about the production meeting.
b. I'm ringing about the accounts meeting.
c. I'm ringing about the marketing meeting.

4D.3 📼

a. Can I <u>take</u> a <u>mess</u>age?
b. I'll <u>tell</u> him you <u>called</u>.
c. Could you <u>ask</u> her to <u>call</u> me?

4E Speaking

4E.1 📼

MESSAGE 1: You have telephoned Q and A Software. There's nobody here to take your call right now. If you'd like to leave your name and your number, we'll call you back. Speak after the tone. Thank you. (beep)

YOU: ....

EXAMPLE: *This is Lana Corning of Wise Electronics. I'd like to speak to Gordon Klein. I'm ringing about our new accounting system. Could he call me before six? My number's one five eight, two one four zero. Thanks.*

MESSAGE 2: This is Santini Distribution, six seven six, four three two. I'm afraid we cannot answer your call just at the moment. Please leave your name and your phone number and we'll contact you as soon as possible. Please speak clearly after you hear the tone. *(beep)*

YOU: ....

EXAMPLE: *This is Lana Corning of Wise Electronics. I'd like to speak to Annie Pastori. I'm ringing about a late delivery – order number two three two one two. Could she call me as soon as possible? My number's one five eight, two one four zero. Thanks.*

MESSAGE 3: You have called the Sumiti Bank on four oh one, six nine two. I'm sorry we're closed at the moment. Our hours of business are from nine-thirty to five-thirty. If you would like to leave a message, speak after you hear the tone. Please speak clearly and leave your name and your telephone number. *(beep)*

YOU: ....

EXAMPLE: *This is Lana Corning of Wise Electronics. I'd like to speak to Kenji Hata. I'm ringing about land investments in the Far East. Could he call me after three? My number's one five eight, two one four zero. Thanks.*

UNIT 5

Schedules

5B Listening

5B.1

a. iii; b. i; c. ii

5B.1 📼

When's the marketing meeting? It's on the third of May.

What's the date of the sales meeting? It's on the first of June.

When's the conference scheduled for? It's on the fifth of March.

5B.2

See 5B.1

5B.3

a. Frankfurt Technology Fair 2nd–7th October; Janet Shields

b. Expotech 12th–14th July; Janet Shields, Peter Dressler and Marc de la Tour

c. ComInTech 6th–10th July; Peter Dressler

d. Sydney AI Fair 18th–23rd September; Janet Shields

e. Infotek 1st–3rd August; nobody

5B.3 📼

PETER DRESSLER: OK. Everybody ready? I wanted to look at the upcoming trade fairs. I've got all the dates here, and I'd like us to decide who's going to each one. Is that OK? Good. First we've got Expotec in Casablanca.

JANET SHIELDS: What are the dates this year, Peter?

PETER DRESSLER: First week of October: from the second to the seventh. You went to that last year, didn't you, Janet?

JANET SHIELDS: That's right.

PETER DRESSLER: Do you want to go again this year?

JANET SHIELDS: Well, I don't mind. Did you say it was October the second to the seventh?

PETER DRESSLER: That's right.

JANET SHIELDS: When's the Sydney AI Fair?

PETER DRESSLER: It's quite late this year; it's in September from the eighteenth to the twenty-third.

JANET SHIELDS: Eighteenth to the twenty-third. Who's going to Sydney this year?

PETER DRESSLER: Well, I was hoping you would. Can I put you down for Sydney and Casablanca?

JANET SHIELDS: Yes. Why not?

PETER DRESSLER: Good. Now, ComInTech in Geneva's from the sixth of July to the tenth. I've got to be in Switzerland on the third and fourth of July, so I thought I'd go straight on to ComInTech.

JANET SHIELDS: OK.

MARC DE LA TOUR: When's Frankfurt scheduled for?

PETER DRESSLER: Frankfurt's from the twelfth to the fourteenth of July, Marc. Now, this is the important one. I think, if possible, we should all be in Frankfurt. Any problems with that?

JANET SHIELDS: No, none at all.

MARC DE LA TOUR: No, fine.

PETER DRESSLER: Good. So we all go to Frankfurt. What does that leave? Oh, yes. InfoTek in San Francisco, which is August the first to August the third. You went to that last year, Janet.

JANET SHIELDS: That's right. I wasn't impressed.

PETER DRESSLER: I remember.

MARC DE LA TOUR: What was wrong with it?

JANET SHIELDS: Terrible organisation, no real buyers to be seen.

PETER DRESSLER: Well, for the time being, let's say that we'll give San Francisco a miss.

MARC DE LA TOUR: So, nobody to San Francisco.

PETER DRESSLER: That's right. Not unless something happens to indicate that it's going to be a bit better than last year.

5C Language check
. . . .

5C.1 📼

The missing prepositions are in **bold**.

a. Expotec starts **on** the second **of** October and finishes **on** the seventh.

b. The Sydney AI Fair is **from** the eighteenth **to** the twenty-third **of** September.

c. ComInTech is **in** July; **from** the sixth **to** the tenth.

5C.2 📼

a. When's the sales meeting? It's on the sixth of December.

b. What's the date of the press conference? It's on the ninth of June.

c. When's the production meeting? It's on the twenty-first of April.

d. When's the conference scheduled for? It's from the first to the fifth of February.

5D Pronunciation
. . . .

5D.3 📼

a. the fourth of September

b. the fifth of August

c. the sixth of July

d. the seventh of June

e. the eighth of May

f. the ninth of April

g. the tenth of March

h. the eleventh of February

i. the twelfth of January

5D.4 📼

a. The production meeting is on the twenty-second of June.

b. The sales meeting is on the fifth of February.

c. The finance meeting is on the fifth of July.

d. The Paris Trade Fair is from the twenty-fifth of April to the third of May.

e. The annual conference is from the thirty-first of September to the fourth of October.

5D.5 📼

a. When's the marketing meeting?

b. What's the date of the sales meeting?

c. When's the conference scheduled for?

5D.7 📼

QUESTION 1: What's the date today?

YOU: ....

QUESTION 2: What was the date yesterday?

YOU: ....

QUESTION 3: What's the date tomorrow?

YOU: ....

QUESTION 4: What's your date of birth?

YOU: ....

QUESTION 5: What are the dates of your holidays this year?

YOU: ....

5E Speaking

5E.1

QUESTION 2: When's the launch of Fotoscan in Europe scheduled for?

YOU: ....

EXAMPLE: *It's on the thirty-first of January.*

QUESTION 3: When's the annual inspection visit?

YOU: ....

EXAMPLE: *It's from the fifteenth to the eighteenth of April.*

QUESTION 4: What's the date of the annual conference?

YOU: ....

EXAMPLE: *It's from the twelfth to the sixteenth of January.*

QUESTION 5: What's the date of the Newport Communications Fair?

YOU: ....

EXAMPLE: *It's from the twenty-first to the twenty-third of January.*

QUESTION 6: What's the date of the regional sales meeting?

YOU: ....

EXAMPLE: *It's on the fourteenth of December.*

QUESTION 7: When's the launch of Fotoscan in Japan scheduled for?

YOU: ....

EXAMPLE: *It's on the twelfth of February.*

UNIT 6

Sales figures

6B Listening

6B.1

France 6A.4

Spain and Portugal 6A.2

UK and Ireland 6A.6

Italy 6A.1

Germany 6A.3

Greece 6A.5

6B.1 📼

The missing words are in **bold**.

JENNY DEWAN: Before we get started, I'd like a brief oral report from everyone on sales in their region. Is that OK? Jacques, how are things going in France?

JACQUES: Not bad. We're **eight per cent up on** last year.

JENNY DEWAN: Good. What about Spain and Portugal, Belinda?

BELINDA: Well, we didn't start the year very well, but sales are **going up** very **rapidly** now.

JENNY DEWAN: Why do you think that is?

BELINDA: We've done a lot more publicity this year, and I think we're beginning to establish our name in the market.

JENNY DEWAN: So you expect sales to continue going up?

BELINDA: I think so, yes.

JENNY DEWAN: Good. Pete. How are things going in the UK?

PETE: About **the same** as last year.

JENNY DEWAN: Are you happy with that?

PETE: Yes. The market's difficult at the moment.

JENNY DEWAN: Giancarlo?

GIANCARLO: Not very good, really. We're **down on** last year: it seems to be a general trend in Italy.

JENNY DEWAN: Aha. How long do you think that'll continue?

GIANCARLO: Difficult to say. Six months, maybe more.

JENNY DEWAN: Well, we'll have to see how it goes. What about the German market, Otto?

OTTO: We've had a good year. At the moment sales are **holding steady**. Christmas was very good this year.

JENNY DEWAN: Yes. Christmas sales were very good. Finally, Terry. How are things in Greece?

TERRY: Well, we're very new in Greece, so sales levels are quite low. But, sales are **going up slowly**. I feel optimistic.

JENNY DEWAN: Excellent. Now I'd just like to remind everyone that …

6B.2

a. $341m

b.

i. $20m; ii. $18m; iii. $40m; iv. $47m

6B.2 📼

JENNY DEWAN: As you all know, we've had a good year for sales: our total sales are three hundred and fifty-two million dollars, which is eleven million up on last year. Christmas was particularly strong this year: six million up on last year, which is very gratifying. The summer market continues to develop and August sales of forty-four million dollars were four million up on last year. It wasn't all good. In March we had sales of eighteen million dollars. March is never a very good month, but this figure was two million down on last year. The rest of the year was fairly typical. May, for example, at almost eighteen million was about the same as last year. Now if we look at the sales by region, we see that in Western Europe …

6C Language check

6C.2 📼

In Spain, sales are going up slowly.

In Germany, sales are going down rapidly.

In Italy, sales are holding steady.

In Japan, sales are going down slowly.

6C.3 📼

In Spain, sales are two hundred and seventy-one thousand dollars down on last year.

In Spain, sales are twelve per cent down on last year.

In Germany, sales are one hundred and six thousand dollars up on last year.

In Germany, sales are four per cent up on last year.

In Italy, sales are two hundred and twenty-nine thousand dollars down on last year.

In Italy, sales are seven per cent down on last year.

In Japan, sales are about the same as last year.

6D Pronunciation

6D.1 📼

nine

eighty-nine

seven hundred and eighty-nine

six thousand, seven hundred and eighty-nine

fifty-six thousand, seven hundred and eighty-nine

four hundred and fifty-six thousand, seven hundred and eighty-nine

three million, four hundred and fifty-six thousand, seven hundred and eighty-nine

twenty-three million, four hundred and fifty-six thousand, seven hundred and eighty-nine

one hundred and twenty-three million, four hundred and fifty-six thousand, seven hundred and eighty-nine

two and a half million

two point five million

two million, five hundred thousand

thirty-three per cent

ten per cent

five per cent

6D.3 📼

a. Sales are about the same as last year.

b. Sales are holding steady.

6E Speaking

6E.1 📼

QUESTION 2: What's the situation in Norway?

YOU: ....

EXAMPLE: *Sales are going down rapidly and we're eight per cent down on last year.*

QUESTION 3: Aha. Oh, well. What about Finland?

YOU: ....

EXAMPLE: *Sales are going up rapidly and we're twelve per cent up on last year.*

QUESTION 4: Oh, that's excellent. How are we doing in Sweden?

YOU: ....

EXAMPLE: *Sales are holding steady and we're about the same as last year.*

QUESTION 5: Well, that's acceptable. What about

the total situation for Scandinavia?

YOU: ....

EXAMPLE: *Sales are going up slowly and we're three per cent up on last year.*

6E.2 🖭

QUESTION 1: What's the situation with inflation in your country?

YOU: ....

QUESTION 2: Really. What about interest rates?

YOU: ....

QUESTION 3: And house prices?

YOU: ....

QUESTION 4: Aha. What about unemployment?

YOU: ....

UNIT 7

Making appointments

7A Preparation

7A 🖭

JOHN WATERMAN: Let me see. I'm meeting Etta Caducci from Unital at two o'clock on Tuesday, and then at four I'm seeing Royce Lowton about this month's production figures. There's a divisional meeting on Wednesday morning at eleven, then I'm having lunch with Andrew Symes. In the afternoon, I'm meeting Harlan Brown from MXS. On Thursday, I'm having lunch with Sue, but I'm free in the morning and the afternoon. On Friday morning, I'm seeing Christina Bunnenberg about the CJK contract.

7B Listening

7B.1

7B.1 🖭

The missing words are in **bold**.

Conversation 1

JOHN WATERMAN: John Waterman.

CHRISTINA BUNNENBERG: John. This is Christina Bunnenberg.

JOHN WATERMAN: Ah, Christina. How are you?

CHRISTINA BUNNENBERG: Fine, thanks. And yourself?

JOHN WATERMAN: Very well. What can I do for you?

CHRISTINA BUNNENBERG: I've just received this report on the CJK contract.

JOHN WATERMAN: Yes. It's rather more complicated than we expected, isn't it?

CHRISTINA BUNNENBERG: It is. I was wondering if we could get together to talk about it.

JOHN WATERMAN: Aren't we meeting on Friday?

CHRISTINA BUNNENBERG: I'd like to see you before that. Can **we meet** tomorrow?

JOHN WATERMAN: I'm afraid I'm **busy** tomorrow. **How about** Thursday?

CHRISTINA BUNNENBERG: Let me see... I'm free in the morning on Thursday. Shall we say half past ten?

JOHN WATERMAN: OK. Half past ten it is. So, I'll see you on Thursday. Bye.

CHRISTINA BUNNENBERG: Bye.

Conversation 2

FRANÇOIS LETELLIER: François Letellier.

JOHN WATERMAN: François. This is John.

FRANÇOIS LETELLIER: Hello, John. How are you?

JOHN WATERMAN: I'm very well, thanks. Listen François, I'm meeting Christina Bunnenberg on Thursday at ten-thirty. It's about the CJK contract.

FRANÇOIS LETELLIER: Well, good luck. You're going to need it.

JOHN WATERMAN: I wonder if I could meet you before that. I've not really had time to have a good look at the figures yet.

MONDAY	TUESDAY	WEDNESDAY	THURSDAY	FRIDAY
		~~11.00: Divisional Meeting~~ 11.00 Christina Bunnenberg	~~10.30 Christina Bunnenberg~~	~~10.00: Christina Bunnenberg (CJK contract)~~ 9.30: Harlan Brown
		12.30: lunch, Andrew Symes	1.00: lunch, Sue Bowlan	
	2.00: Etta Caducci (Unital) 4.00: Royce Lowton (production figures)	~~2.30 Harlan Brown (MXS)~~ 2.00 François Letellier		

FRANÇOIS LETELLIER: Certainly. When would you like to meet?

JOHN WATERMAN: What are **you doing** tomorrow morning at nine?

FRANÇOIS LETELLIER: Tomorrow morning is impossible, I'm afraid. **Can we meet** in the afternoon?

JOHN WATERMAN: That's a bit difficult for me. I've got the divisional meeting at eleven, I'm having lunch with Andrew Symes and somebody from MXS is coming in the afternoon.

FRANÇOIS LETELLIER: Can't you put off the meeting with MXS?

JOHN WATERMAN: I suppose I could.

FRANÇOIS LETELLIER: Then we could meet tomorrow after lunch, say about two o'clock.

JOHN WATERMAN: OK, great. I'll have to ring MXS first: can I call you later to confirm?

FRANÇOIS LETELLIER: Sure. No problem.

JOHN WATERMAN: Right you are. Bye.

FRANÇOIS LETELLIER: Bye.

Conversation 3

RECEPTIONIST: Can I help you?

JOHN WATERMAN: Can I speak to Harlan Brown, please?

RECEPTIONIST: Who's calling?

JOHN WATERMAN: This is John Waterman from Hearst Behring.

RECEPTIONIST: One moment, please.

HARLAN BROWN: Hello, John. What can I do for you?

JOHN WATERMAN: Hello, Harlan. It's about our meeting at two-thirty tomorrow. I'm afraid I can't make it. Something's come up.

HARLAN BROWN: Oh, that's a pity. Can **we meet at** another time? I'm **free on** Friday morning.

JOHN WATERMAN: Friday morning. Just a minute... Fine. What time?

HARLAN BROWN: Nine-thirty?

JOHN WATERMAN: Right. Friday morning at nine-thirty. Thanks very much.

HARLAN BROWN: See you on Friday.

JOHN WATERMAN: Yes, see you then. Bye.

HARLAN BROWN: Bye.

Conversation 4

CHRISTINA BUNNENBERG: John?

JOHN WATERMAN: Christina. How are you?

CHRISTINA BUNNENBERG: I'm fine. John, were you going to the divisional meeting tomorrow morning?

JOHN WATERMAN: Er, yes. Why?

CHRISTINA BUNNENBERG: Did you know it's been cancelled?

JOHN WATERMAN: No, no, I didn't.

CHRISTINA BUNNENBERG: I just got a fax five minutes ago.

JOHN WATERMAN: Ah.

CHRISTINA BUNNENBERG: That means we can bring forward our Thursday meeting to Wednesday morning.

JOHN WATERMAN: Oh, good, good.

CHRISTINA BUNNENBERG: Can **you come** to my office at about eleven?

JOHN WATERMAN: Eleven. Yes, fine. OK. **See you** tomorrow.

CHRISTINA BUNNENBERG: See you tomorrow. Bye.

JOHN WATERMAN: Bye. Oh no.

7C *Language check*
....

7C.1 🔲

The missing prepositions are in **bold**.

a. Today I'm having lunch **with** Joe Gianelli.

b. Tomorrow morning **at** ten I'm going **to** a sales meeting.

c. I'm visiting the factory **on** Wednesday **in** the morning.

d. **At** eight a.m. **on** Friday I'm flying **to** Paris **for** a training course.

7C.2 🔲

a. Tomorrow I'm having lunch in La Tour d'Or with a client.

b. On Wednesday, I'm going to Budapest for a trade fair.

c. I'm staying at the Intercontinental on Wednesday night.

d. On Thursday, I'm meeting Maria Csemi.

e. On Friday, I'm flying to Mexico for a holiday.

7D *Pronunciation*
....

7D.3 🔲

a. I'm <u>fly</u>ing to New <u>York</u> on <u>Mon</u>day.

b. I'm <u>hav</u>ing <u>lunch</u> with Mr <u>Bak</u>er on <u>Tues</u>day.

c. I'm <u>meet</u>ing Mr <u>Helms</u> on <u>Wednes</u>day.

d. I'm a<u>fraid</u> I'm <u>busy</u> on <u>Thurs</u>day.

e. I'm <u>free</u> on <u>Fri</u>day <u>morn</u>ing.

7E Speaking

7E.1 📼

QUESTION 2: What are you doing on Monday afternoon?

YOU: ....

EXAMPLE: *I'm flying to Amsterdam for a trade fair.*

QUESTION 3: Are you free on Tuesday?

YOU: ....

EXAMPLE: *No, I'm going to the trade fair.*

QUESTION 4: Can we meet for lunch on Wednesday?

YOU: ....

EXAMPLE: *No, I'm having lunch with Bill Canning.*

QUESTION 5: Are you free on Thursday morning at ten?

YOU: ....

EXAMPLE: *No, I'm visiting a factory.*

QUESTION 6: What about Thursday afternoon?

YOU: ....

EXAMPLE: *I'm going to a meeting at ICL.*

QUESTION 7: Are you free for lunch on Friday?

YOU: ....

EXAMPLE: *No, I'm having lunch with Joanne from ICL.*

QUESTION 8: What are you doing at three in the afternoon on Friday?

YOU: ....

EXAMPLE: *I'm finishing work early.*

7E.2 📼

JOHN WATERMAN: … right so, can we meet on Monday morning?

CLIENT: I'm afraid I'm busy on Monday.

JOHN WATERMAN: How about Tuesday?

CLIENT: I'm going to the trade fair in Amsterdam. Are you free on Wednesday afternoon?

JOHN WATERMAN: I'm afraid not. How about Friday morning? Are you free?

CLIENT: Yes, I am. How about ten o'clock?

JOHN WATERMAN: Fine. See you on Friday then.

CLIENT: See you on Friday. Goodbye.

JOHN WATERMAN: Goodbye.

7E.4 📼

QUESTION 1: What are you doing on Monday morning?

YOU: ....

QUESTION 2: Are you free on Monday afternoon at three?

YOU: ....

QUESTION 3: How about Tuesday morning at nine?

YOU: ....

QUESTION 4: What are you doing on Tuesday afternoon?

YOU: ....

QUESTION 5: Are you free on Wednesday at two?

YOU: ....

QUESTION 6: What are you doing on Thursday at ten?

YOU: ....

QUESTION 7: How about Thursday afternoon at two?

YOU: ....

QUESTION 8: Can we meet on Friday at six?

YOU: ....

UNIT 8

Prices and discounts

8A Preparation

8A.2

a. v; b. i; c. iv; d. ii; e. iii

8B Listening

8B.1 📼

a. two weeks

b. senior managers

c. English

8B.2

a. 8.30 – 12.30, 1.30 – 6.30, five days a week

b. will send information

c. $1,200 (including VAT)

d. yes, $980

e. no, but with five participants one place is free

f. thirty days, 3 per cent discount for payment within ten days

g. hotel

h. 3rd – 14th April

i. 15th March

8B.2 📼

The missing words are in **bold**.

RECEPTIONIST: Executive Education Programs. Good morning, can I help you?

CAROL PARRY: Good morning. I'd like some information about one of your courses.

RECEPTIONIST: What's the name of the course?

CAROL PARRY: Strategic Management in Global Markets.

RECEPTIONIST: Just one moment, putting you through.

TOM ATKINSON: Tom Atkinson speaking. What can I do for you?

CAROL PARRY: Good morning. This is Carol Parry of Locke-Burnett. I've seen an advertisement for one of your courses: Strategic Management in Global Markets.

TOM ATKINSON: Ah, yes.

CAROL PARRY: I'd like some information.

TOM ATKINSON: Certainly.

CAROL PARRY: **What's the** timetable of the course?

TOM ATKINSON: Well, it's extremely intensive. We start at eight-thirty, there's a break for lunch at twelve-thirty for one hour and then we continue until six-thirty in the evening.

CAROL PARRY: So that's nine hours a day?

TOM ATKINSON: That's correct. There are also assignments to do in the evenings, which adds another five hours a week.

CAROL PARRY: Five days a week or six?

TOM ATKINSON: Five.

CAROL PARRY: **Can you tell me about** the content of the course?

TOM ATKINSON: I can do better than that: I can send you a full course program so that you can see exactly what your managers will be studying.

CAROL PARRY: Excellent. **Can you tell me** the price per participant?

TOM ATKINSON: It's one thousand two hundred dollars.

CAROL PARRY: **Does that** include VAT?

TOM ATKINSON: Yes, it does.

CAROL PARRY: **Do you have** a price for company clients?

TOM ATKINSON: Yes, we do. If the participant's company is paying for the course, the price is nine hundred and eighty dollars.

CAROL PARRY: And if I send three people on the course, **can you offer me** a discount?

TOM ATKINSON: Not for three people, no. But if you send five, one place is free.

CAROL PARRY: That's interesting. **What are** your terms of payment?

TOM ATKINSON: Thirty days. If you pay within ten days, there's a three per cent discount.

CAROL PARRY: Fine. **What about** accommodation? **Do you** arrange that?

TOM ATKINSON: We book hotel rooms for you. That's no problem.

CAROL PARRY: Good, fine. Dates. **Can you tell me** the dates of the next course?

TOM ATKINSON: The next course is in April, from the third to the fourteenth.

CAROL PARRY: **Are there** still places?

TOM ATKINSON: At the moment, yes.

CAROL PARRY: **What's the** deadline for reserving places?

TOM ATKINSON: The fifteenth of March. Would you like me to send you some booking forms with the information?

CAROL PARRY: Yes, please.

TOM ATKINSON: Can you give me your address?

CAROL PARRY: Yes, my name's Carol Parry. That's P–A–double R …

8C Language check

8C.1

a. I'd like some information about one of your products.

b. I'd like some information about one of your services.

8C.2

The order of the sentences is: b; d; a; c

8C.3

a. If you pay within ten days, there's a two and a half per cent discount.

b. If you buy ten, one's free.

c. If you pay cash, the price is one hundred and fifty pounds.

d. If you spend a hundred dollars or more, there's a six per cent discount.

8C.5

a. Can you tell me the/your name?

b. Can you tell me the time?

c. Can you tell me the date?

d. Can you tell me the/your phone number?

e. Can you tell me the/your address?

8C.6

a. Does that include service?

b. Does that include transport?

8C.7

b. is not correct

8D Pronunciation

8D.1

a. seven point five per cent.

b. twelve months

c. thirty days

d. one thousand, two hundred and fifty pounds
e. nine hundred and eighty dollars
f. the twelfth of April
g. two point five per cent
h. one hundred and fifty pounds
i. six per cent
j. three five seven   six five one two
k. eight thirty
l. the sixteen of August

8D.3 🔲

a. <u>How</u> <u>much</u> does it <u>cost</u>?
b. <u>What</u>'s the <u>price</u>?
c. Do you <u>have</u> a <u>price</u> for <u>company</u> <u>clients</u>?
d. <u>What</u> are your <u>terms</u> of <u>payment</u>?

8E Speaking

8E.1 🔲

QUESTION 2: Do you have a special price for company clients?
YOU: ....
EXAMPLE: *Yes, it's four hundred and ninety-nine dollars.*
QUESTION 3: If I buy ten, is there a discount?
YOU: ....
EXAMPLE: *Yes, there's a ten per cent discount.*
QUESTION 4: Is there a discount if I pay within fifteen days?
YOU: ....
EXAMPLE: Yes, there's a two and a half per cent discount.

8E.2 🔲

RECEPTIONIST: Q and A Software. Good morning, can I help you?
CUSTOMER: Good morning. I'd like some information about one of your products.
RECEPTIONIST: Just one moment, putting you through.
SALES REPRESENTATIVE: Sales department. Can I help you?
CUSTOMER: Good morning. I'd like some information about Pro-Word.
SALES REPRESENTATIVE: What would you like to know?
CUSTOMER: Can you tell me the price?
SALES REPRESENTATIVE: It's five hundred and thirty dollars.
CUSTOMER: Does that include VAT?
SALES REPRESENTATIVE: Yes, it does.
CUSTOMER: Do you have a price for company clients?

SALES REPRESENTATIVE: Yes, we do: it's four hundred and ninety-nine dollars.
CUSTOMER: If I buy ten, can you offer me a discount?
SALES REPRESENTATIVE: Yes, we can give you ten per cent.
CUSTOMER: What are your terms of payment?
SALES REPRESENTATIVE: Thirty days. If you pay within fifteen days, there's a two and a half per cent discount.

UNIT 9

Company profiles

9A Preparation

9A.2

a. based
b. value
c. turnover
d. profits
e. employees

9B Listening

9B.1

a. UK; Germany
b. £31m
c. £3.2m
d. £48.5m
e. 148

9B.1 🔲

GENERAL MANAGER: Right. Everybody ready? Good. Before we look at the figures in detail, I'd like to outline some of the facts about Cerico. As you know, we are located in Seville, in Spain. The main activity of the company is exporting traditional hand-painted ceramics from all over Spain. We are also involved in manufacturing through Ceramicas Rodas in Granada, a subsidiary of Cerico. Our customers, in the main, are department stores and furniture shops, and our main markets are the UK and Germany. We are particularly strong in the UK, where we have a lot of contacts. We are selective in what we choose to export: our image is one of good taste and high quality.

We have one hundred and forty-eight employees in Spain, Britain and Germany, of whom eighty are representatives paid mainly on a commission basis. In the last financial year our turnover was over thirty-one million pounds with pre-tax profits of three point two million pounds. The total value of the company is forty-eight point five million pounds.

9C Language check

9C.2

The missing words are in **bold**.

a. Where is your company **based**?
b. How many **employees** are there?
c. What was your company's **turnover**?
d. What were your company's **profits**?
e. What's the **value** of the company?

9C.3

a. What's the main activity of the company?
b. Where's the company located?
c. What are the company's main markets?

9D Pronunciation

9D.2

a. five hundred and sixty-seven employees
b. eighteen offices
c. thirteen countries
d. eighty-seven point five million dollars
e. seven point nine million dollars
f. three hundred and sixty-five million dollars

9E Speaking

9E.1

QUESTION 1: What's the main activity of the company?
YOU: ....
EXAMPLE: *Designing and selling software.*
QUESTION 2: What are the main country markets?
YOU: ....
EXAMPLE: *Great Britain and the USA.*
QUESTION 3: How many employees are there?
YOU: ....
EXAMPLE: *Eighty-seven.*
QUESTION 4: What's the turnover?
YOU: ....

EXAMPLE: *Just over eleven and a half million pounds.*
QUESTION 5: What are the pre-tax profits?
YOU: ....
EXAMPLE: *One point six five million pounds.*
QUESTION 6: What's the value of the company?
YOU: ....
EXAMPLE: *Twenty-one million pounds.*

9E.2

YOU: ....
MANAGING DIRECTOR: In Oxford.
YOU: ....
MANAGING DIRECTOR: Designing and selling software.
YOU: ....
MANAGING DIRECTOR: Great Britain and the USA.
YOU: ....
MANAGING DIRECTOR: Eighty-seven.
YOU: ....
MANAGING DIRECTOR: Just over eleven and a half million pounds.
YOU: ....
MANAGING DIRECTOR: One point six five million pounds.
YOU: ....
MANAGING DIRECTOR: Twenty-one million pounds.

UNIT 10

Business trips

10A Preparation

10A.1

1. do	6. took
2. went	7. get
3. have	8. could
4. said	9. give
5. tell	10. thought

10B Listening

10B.1

a. France and Germany
b. two weeks

I0B.I 📼

HANS MULLER: Janet! Where were you last week?

JANET BRYAN: Oh, I was away.

HANS MULLER: Where did you go?

JANET BRYAN: France and Germany to see clients.

HANS MULLER: Sounds nice.

JANET BRYAN: Oh, it was hard work, I'll tell you.

HANS MULLER: How long were you away?

JANET BRYAN: Two weeks.

I0B.2

The order arrived late and part of the order was missing.

I0B.2 📼

RECEPTIONIST: B and D White. Can I help you?

TIM MCBRIDE: Oh, hello. This is Tim McBride from PC Solutions. Can I speak to the sales department?

RECEPTIONIST: One moment. Putting you through.

SALES REPRESENTATIVE: Sales department.

TIM MCBRIDE: Hello. This is Tim McBride from PC Solutions. There's a bit of a problem with our last order.

SALES REPRESENTATIVE: Oh dear. What exactly is the problem?

TIM MCBRIDE: Well, it was two weeks late for a start.

SALES REPRESENTATIVE: But you've got it now?

TIM MCBRIDE: Not exactly. Part of the order is missing.

SALES REPRESENTATIVE: Really?

TIM MCBRIDE: Yes. The three eight sixes arrived, but there are no four eight sixes in the package although the two hundred I ordered are here on the delivery note.

SALES REPRESENTATIVE: Oh, I'm sorry. I'll check it out and ring you back in half an hour.

TIM MCBRIDE: OK.

SALES REPRESENTATIVE: Bye.

TIM MCBRIDE: Bye.

I0B.3

a. 7.30
b. Berlin

I0B.3 📼

JOHN LUCAS: Marie-Noëlle!

MARIE-NOËLLE COUSIN: John! How nice of you to meet me.

JOHN LUCAS: Not at all. Did you have a good flight?

MARIE-NOËLLE COUSIN: Oh, not bad.

JOHN LUCAS: What time did you leave Prague?

MARIE-NOËLLE COUSIN: Half past seven.

JOHN LUCAS: Half past seven!

MARIE-NOËLLE COUSIN: Yes. We had to change planes in Berlin and it was a six-hour wait.

JOHN LUCAS: Oh, you poor thing. Let's get a taxi.

10C Language check

I0C.I 📼

The missing words are in **bold**.

On Monday I **met** Terry Marsden of CFG in the morning and **had** lunch with Françoise Dulac. I **flew** to Manchester on Tuesday and **went** to the regional marketing meeting. I **slept** at the Manchester City Hilton and **came** back the next day. On Thursday I **read** Jerry Tyson's report and **wrote** the notes for my presentation. On Friday I **took** a train to Brighton and **gave** the presentation to the directors of Selby and Bonham. On the way home I **bought** some flowers for Alison.

I0C.2 📼

a. Who did you have lunch with on Monday?
b. Where did you go on Tuesday?
c. Why did you go to Manchester?
d. What time did you fly back to London?
e. What did you do on Tuesday morning?
f. What did you buy for Alison?

10D Pronunciation

I0D.2 📼

a. <u>What</u> <u>time</u> did you <u>leave</u> <u>Prague</u>?
b. Did you <u>have</u> to <u>change</u> <u>planes</u>?
c. <u>Who</u> did you <u>fly</u> <u>with</u>?

10E Speaking

I0E.I 📼

CLIENT: Hello! How kind of you to meet me.

SALES MANAGER: Not at all. Did you have a good flight?

CLIENT: Yes, thank you very much. Very good.

SALES MANAGER: What time did you leave London?

CLIENT: Seven o'clock this morning.

SALES MANAGER: Who did you fly with?

CLIENT: Lufthansa.

SALES MANAGER: Did you have to change planes?

CLIENT: No, no I didn't.

10E.3 📟

COLLEAGUE: I didn't see you last week. Where were you?
YOU: ....
COLLEAGUE: Where did you go?
YOU: ....
COLLEAGUE: Ah. How long were you away?
YOU: ....

Example conversation

COLLEAGUE A: I didn't see you last week. Where were you?
COLLEAGUE B: I was away on a business trip.
COLLEAGUE A: Where did you go?
COLLEAGUE B: The States: New York, Chicago and San Francisco.
COLLEAGUE A: Ah. How long were you away?
COLLEAGUE B: Two weeks.

10E.4 📟

TONY LAW: B and D White. Can I help you?
YOU: ....
TONY LAW: Speaking.
YOU: ....
TONY LAW: Oh, hello. What can I do for you?
YOU: ....
TONY LAW: Oh, I'm sorry. I'll check it and ring you back later.

Example conversation

TONY LAW: B and D White. Can I help you?
DOMINIC MARTIN: Could I speak to Tony Law, please.
TONY LAW: Speaking.
DOMINIC MARTIN: Oh, hello. This is Dominic Martin from AFL.
TONY LAW: Oh, hello. What can I do for you?
DOMINIC MARTIN: We received two hundred bearings from you this morning, but they're the wrong type. I wanted three millimetre not four millimetre bearings.
TONY LAW: Oh, I'm sorry. I'll check it and ring you back later.

10E.5 📟

QUESTION 1: What did you do on Monday?
YOU: ....
QUESTION 2: What did you do on Tuesday?
YOU: ....
QUESTION 3: What did you do on Wednesday?
YOU: ....
QUESTION 4: What did you do on Thursday?
YOU: ....
QUESTION 5: What did you do on Friday?
YOU: ....

UNIT 11

Instructions

11A Preparation

11A.1

The machine is an automatic cash dispenser or cash machine (US English: automatic teller).

11B Listening

11B.1

1.b (a computer); 2.a (a VCR); 3.d (a car)

11B.1 📟

Instruction 1
OK. You turn on the CPU with this big button here, the one on the front marked POWER, and you turn on the monitor with the little switch down here under the screen. Wait a few seconds … and there you are.

Instruction 2
It's easy. Put the cassette in at the front here, just push it gently, the machine'll take it in. Right, that's it. Now, get the remote control, turn on the TV and set the channel to ZERO. OK. Now, move the little switch on the top of the remote control … that's it … the red one, move that to VCR. OK. Hit play, and it starts. If you want to rewind …

Instruction 3
Make sure you're comfortable. OK. First of all, check you're in neutral: take the gear lever in your hand and see if you can move it from left to right. If the car's in neutral it should move fairly freely … good. Turn the key in the ignition and press down slightly on the accelerator, good … Now, press down on the clutch, no, no, the clutch, that one there … that's it. Good. Take the gear lever again and put the car in first: left and forward, left and forward, good. Right, now, at the same time as you …

11B.2

Name	Hart Components
Address	19 Barracks Hill London SW19
Tel:	(81) 218 9098
Fax:	(81) 218 7632
Dates of visits	26/7
Contact name	John Lord
Position	Distribution Manager
Decision maker	yes /(no)

If no

Name of decision maker	David Hart
Position of decision maker	General Manager
Initiated by	(client) / ALC

11B.2 📼

DOMINIC LASALLE: Juliet?

JULIET LEHAM: Aha?

DOMINIC LASALLE: Can you give me a hand with this?

JULIET LEHAM: With what?

DOMINIC LASALLE: Oh, this report card. It's that sales visit to Hart Components.

JULIET LEHAM: Sure. Let's have a look. Name, Hart Components, address, nineteen Barracks Hill S–W–nineteen, telephone, yes, fax...good. Looks OK so far. Now, in DATE you put the date of the visit. When was it?

DOMINIC LASALLE: This morning.

JULIET LEHAM: Today's the …

DOMINIC LASALLE: Twenty-sixth.

JULIET LEHAM: So here, in the first box, you put twenty-sixth of July, twenty-six seven. Right, contact name. That's the name of the person you saw. Who did you talk to in the company?

DOMINIC LASALLE: John Lord.

JULIET LEHAM: Oh, John Lord. I know him. OK. So in CONTACT NAME you put John Lord. Good. Position, that's his job. What's he doing now?

DOMINIC LASALLE: He's the Distribution Manager.

JULIET LEHAM: Oh, well done, John. OK. Write Distribution Manager in the box called POSITION. Now, can he make a decision to buy or does he need approval?

DOMINIC LASALLE: No, he can't. He was just getting information.

JULIET LEHAM: So, where it says DECISION MAKER you put a circle around NO. Good. Who can make a decision? What's the name of the person who can say yes?

DOMINIC LASALLE: The General Manager, David Hart.

JULIET LEHAM: Right SO NAME OF DECISION MAKER is …

DOMINIC LASALLE: David Hart.

JULIET LEHAM: Aha. And POSITION OF DECISION MAKER is …

DOMINIC LASALLE: General Manager.

JULIET LEHAM: Good. Right. Lastly, initiation. Did they call us or did we call them?

DOMINIC LASALLE: They called us.

JULIET LEHAM: Right. Put a circle around CLIENT, and you've finished the first part.

DOMINIC LASALLE: Thanks very much.

JULIET LEHAM: Don't mention it. Now you've got to do the detailed report which …

11C Language check

11C.1

The missing verbs are in **bold**.

Put in the cassette at the front of the VCR. **Turn on** the TV and **set** the channel to *zero*. **Move** the switch on the top of the remote control to *VCR*. **Press** *play*, and it starts.

11C.2

The order of sentences is d; g; a; e; f; c; b

11C.2 📼

Check you're in neutral. Turn the key in the ignition and press the accelerator to start the engine. Press the clutch. Put the car in first. Press the accelerator slowly. At the same time, release the clutch and release the handbrake.

11C.3 📼

a. When you see SELECT OPERATION, choose WITHDRAW CASH.

b. When you see ENTER AMOUNT, type the amount of money you want and press CONFIRM.

11C.4 📼

a. Where it says ATTENTION, put the name of the person you are sending the fax to.

b. Where it says FROM, put your name.

c. Where it says DATE, put the date.

d. Where it says PAGES, put the total number of pages in the fax.

11D Pronunciation

11D.2 📼

a. When you see ENTER PIN, type your personal identification number.

b. <u>When</u> you <u>see</u> S<small>ELECT</small> O<small>PERATION</small>, <u>choose</u> **withdraw cash**.

c. <u>When</u> you <u>see</u> E<small>NTER</small> A<small>MOUNT</small>, <u>type</u> the <u>amount</u> of <u>money</u> you <u>want</u> and <u>press</u> **confirm**.

11E Speaking

11E.1 🖭

1. Where it says P<small>AY</small>, put the name of the person you're paying the money to. On the second line, write the amount of money in words. You write the amount of money again, in figures, in the box on the right. At the top you put the date, and then you sign it at the bottom.

2. Put the document in here. Wait until it engages. When the light comes on, dial the number.

3. Check your mirror and brake to slow down. Stop at the side of the road. Check the road is clear. Put the car in first. Turn the steering wheel to the left and drive to the other side of the road. Press the clutch and put the car in reverse. Turn the steering wheel to the right and reverse back across the road. Press the clutch and put the car in first again. Turn the steering wheel to the left and complete the turn.

UNIT 12

Competition

12B Listening

12B.1

a. ACE

b. ACE

c. ACE

12B.1 🖭

CONSULTANT: How would you compare yourself with StarLinea? Your products are considerably more expensive than theirs, aren't they?

LAUREN KIER: ACE products are more expensive, but I think they're better value for money. We're a better quality company. Our products are better …

CONSULTANT: Hm. StarLinea's market share's going up.

LAUREN KIER: But we've still got a larger share of the market than they have and a higher turnover.

CONSULTANT: That's true. But, on the other hand …

12B.2

The white bars represent Starlinea, the grey bars ACE.

12B.2 🖭

CONSULTANT: I've got some information here about ACE and StarLinea and how your income breaks down. The three most interesting figures are here on this chart.

LAUREN KIER: OK.

CONSULTANT: Look at the figure for research and development.

LAUREN KIER: Yes, we spend a lot on R and D. That's what this company's about.

CONSULTANT: Perhaps. The fact is, your R and D budget is a lot higher than StarLinea's.

LAUREN KIER: And their advertising budget's very high …

CONSULTANT: Much higher than yours. And look at the levels of profit.

LAUREN KIER: Aha.

CONSULTANT: It's not just the percentage profit that's higher: the actual amount of profit is higher in StarLinea than in ACE, on a lower level of turnover. What I propose first of all is …

12C Language check

12C.1

a. cheap, high, large, low, quick

b. economical, expensive, profitable

The corrected words are in **bold**.

c. Graphic is **cheaper** than Q.Print.

d. Q.Print is less **profitable** than Graphic.

e. Graphic's turnover is larger **than** Q.Print's.

f. The quality of Graphic's work is **better**.

12C.2

a. Tokyo is bigger than Marseilles.

b. A Porsche is faster than a Volvo.

c. The Hilton is more expensive than the Holiday Inn.

d. The Empire State Building is taller than the Eiffel Tower.

e. Saving is more difficult than spending.

12C.3 🖭

a. ACE's turnover is higher than StarLinea's.

b. ACE is less profitable than StarLinea.

c. ACE's R and D budget is higher than StarLinea's.

d. ACE's advertising budget is lower than StarLinea's.

e. ACE's products are better quality than StarLinea's.

f. ACE's products are more expensive than StarLinea's.

12D Pronunciation

12D.2

a. ACE's market share is larger than StarLinea's.

b. ACE's turnover is higher than StarLinea's.

c. ACE is less profitable than StarLinea.

d. ACE's R and D budget is higher than StarLinea's.

e. ACE's advertising budget is lower than StarLinea's.

f. ACE's products are better quality than StarLinea's.

g. ACE's products are more expensive than StarLinea's.

12E Speaking

12E.1 🖭

JOURNALIST: You're having problems with StarLinea at the moment, aren't you?

LAUREN KIER: I don't think we're having real problems. Our share of the market's larger than StarLinea's, our turnover's higher.

JOURNALIST: But StarLinea's more profitable.

LAUREN KIER: Our profits are lower, that's true. That's because our R and D budget's a lot higher.

JOURNALIST: Your products are more expensive than StarLinea's.

LAUREN KIER: Yes, they are. That's because the quality is better.

12E.3 🖭

JOURNALIST: What is the name of your company?

YOU: ....

JOURNALIST: Who do you think is your main competitor?

YOU: ....

JOURNALIST: Are their products better than yours or worse?

YOU: ....

JOURNALIST: What about price?

YOU: ....

JOURNALIST: And market share?

YOU: ....

JOURNALIST: Which company is more profitable?

YOU: ....

JOURNALIST: Why?

YOU: ....